About the Author

Anita Hamilton is a Communications, Leadership and Organisational Change Consultant. She has spent most of her career in senior roles in the media and in communications, working with some of the world's best-known brands. Anita received a BSc (Hons) in Human Psychology and, thirty-six years later, returned to university, gaining a Master of Science in Organisational and Social Psychology at the London School of Economics and Political Science (LSE). Her experiences at LSE inspired this, her first book. Anita continues to consult with leading brands and lectures on communications, strategy and leadership. She is on the Board of Trustees for Advance, the charity for women affected by domestic abuse and those in the criminal justice system. She lives in London with husband Michael and two children, Jack and Alexis.

How to Be a Happy Woman in Mid-Life

Anita Hamilton

How to Be a Happy Woman in Mid-Life

Olympia Publishers
London

www.olympiapublishers.com
OLYMPIA PAPERBACK EDITION

Copyright © Anita Hamilton 2022

A CIP catalogue record for this title is
available from the British Library.

ISBN: 978-1-80074-146-1

First Published in 2022

Olympia Publishers
Tallis House
2 Tallis Street
London
EC4Y 0AB

Printed in Great Britain

Dedication

For Michael, Jack and Alexis, with thanks for your constant support.

Acknowledgements

Firstly, I want to thank my husband Michael who urged me to apply to LSE and fulfil an ambition I'd had for more than a decade. It was a life-changing experience which inspired me to write this book. Michael supported and encouraged me, as he has done throughout my career, while I juggled full-time study and a busy work schedule. He is a news journalist, and his clarity of thought and ability to cut to the core of any issue is invaluable.

I'd like to thank everyone at LSE, from the academics to the students and support staff who were welcoming and friendly from my first day as the oldest student on the course (and probably on campus) through to dissertations and beyond.

I need to single out a few individuals. I thank Dr Lucia Garcia-Lorenzo, and Dr Tom Reader, Programme Directors of MSc Organisational and Social Psychology. I remember speaking with Lucia on the first day at LSE to thank her for accepting me on the course. Her reply was unequivocal, saying that women of my age and experience have much to contribute which was a boost to my confidence from the outset. Tom was hugely influential in helping to develop my thinking, and quietly encouraging as I expressed ideas and concepts. Professor Paul Dolan, the renowned expert on happiness, behaviour and public policy, taught the happiness course at LSE which stimulated many of the ideas and helped to develop my thinking in this book. Dr Cathy Nicholson taught qualitative research techniques and encouraged a new love of investigation and enquiry, skills that I used in researching this book and that I now use in my work life.

I want to thank my fellow students who came to London to study from all over the world, from a diverse range of cultures and backgrounds. Everyone, whether in their twenties, or in the more mature cohort, were generous with friendship and time. I enjoyed the conversations, the debates, belonging.

I particularly want to thank the many dozens of women I interviewed as part of my research. Some of their stories were deeply sad, others uplifting and admirable. Everyone talked to me honestly, openly and bravely. I am confident I have captured the facts of your experience. I trust I have also captured your spirit—your courage, your resilience and your hope.

Thanks also to Paul Hackett, for the cover image.

Finally, I want to thank my mother, Inga, who encouraged me to study psychology as an undergraduate leading to a lifelong interest in human behaviour. And my son, Jack and daughter, Alexis, who spent hours talking with me around the dinner table at home about my ideas. They encouraged me to write this book and helped to convince me that I have something meaningful to say.

Foreword

At the time I was completing this book, the world became engulfed in the coronavirus pandemic. This rapidly changed the way that many of us were living our lives on a day-to-day basis. Being locked down—the policy response of governments to protect its citizens and prevent the spread of this highly contagious virus—put most lives on hold. Some have struggled with these restrictions. Studies have already shown increases in mental health issues, loneliness, and despair. Never before has the simple question—what makes us happy—been brought into such sharp relief.

As the world emerges from the pandemic and life returns to something resembling what was previously known as normal, it is more important than ever that women in mid-life ask themselves what makes them happy. And they develop the confidence to take action to *be* happy. I make the point in the book that despite some populist theories, it is difficult to *think* yourself happy. If lockdowns have taught us nothing else, it is that normal life can be exciting, wonderful, and joyous. A simple hug, time with friends and family, human interaction—all the little things we took for granted are essential to our well-being. As we emerge from lockdown and the restrictions that have brought lives to a standstill, don't wait to make changes. Seize the opportunity to review what makes you happy or more contented. Act now.

There's nothing like fear of death to make people change behaviour, but it's not always simple or straightforward.

Governments across the world, advised by scientists, virologists and the World Health Organisation, recommended that people should stay away from one another to prevent the virus from spreading. Governments quickly implemented a series of fines and/or a permissions system to reinforce the notion that only permitted behaviour outside the home would be tolerated. The levels of compliance differed country to country and, at times, age group by age group. Some were particularly unhappy about their civil liberties being curtailed.

Regardless of these differences, the impact of on individuals, particularly the lack of human contact, increasingly became part of the media narrative and drove much social media conversation. As it became clear that older people were most at risk from the virus, they were shielded as much as possible from human contact. The United Nations published a policy paper in May 2020 highlighting the effects of Covid-19 on older populations specifically raising the effects on mental health for older persons from living alone and physical distancing. As I will explain in this book, social relationships and contact with other people are fundamental to our well-being.

Many of us relied on video calls and social media to maintain contact with others through the pandemic. Can you really substitute face-to-face contact with electronic communication? Is working from home preferable regardless of your age? I argue that while these questions are for everyone, they are particularly critical for women in mid-life. Why? Women in mid-life, pre-pandemic, often faced issues of isolation as children leave home, when bereavement or divorce are more common, and careers hit a plateau or near their end. A common complaint among women is this age group is that they increasingly feel invisible and, sadly, irrelevant. That was before the pandemic when we experienced periods of lockdown. Women in this age group are now a year or more older, with further distance between them and what they may have believed were their most productive years. It is more important that women in mid-life emerge from the pandemic determined to be happy. It may mean making changes, and it may take courage.

Many women with jobs may have been on furlough or faced redundancy. Hopefully, they can return to work or find new opportunities. Many companies are experiencing difficult times meaning that some businesses will fail, while others will be going through massive disruption and transformation. These changes alone put real stress on individuals. Much has been said and written about the damage to the lives of children and young people—education interrupted, fewer jobs and a challenging employment market for graduates. It is right that much of this focus is on the impact on the young. What has largely been ignored is the impact on those in mid-life, and women in particular. My book is a voice speaking for and to this group, as I feel that we need to be seen, to be heard, to be happy.

The pandemic has also shone a spotlight on another essential ingredient for happiness in mid-life—exercise. Some countries stopped all outside activity for months and placed strict limits allowing only essential shopping or restricted exercise. For those people without a garden or balcony this is especially hard. We thrive outside and we need sunlight for our health. Moreover, exercise alleviates many of the symptoms of menopause by helping to relieve stress and help manage weight gain and muscle loss. More of this can be found in the chapter about Health and Happiness.

The pandemic highlights how physical resilience can vary; the coronavirus affects different age groups with different levels of severity. The older you are, the more likely it is to make you seriously ill or possibly kill you. However, psychological resilience—loosely defined as the capacity for individuals to adapt and recover quickly from difficulties or challenges, such as personal tragedy or trauma—is not necessarily age-related. Women in mid-life can and should develop resilience to support their later years. More on this later in this book.

How to be a Happy Woman in Mid-life was a subject close to my heart before the pandemic, and something I am more passionately interested in as we emerge from its effects. This book is based on cutting-edge research and interviews with dozens of women. The challenges women may face in the years after fifty may differ, but the underlying issues and the means to respond are shared. I explore what you can do to be happy in mid-life. It is possible that women in mid-life are entering what could be the most productive, exciting period of their lives. A time of renewal, a time of achievement, a time of happiness.

Chapter 1
What is happiness and why is it important?

Being happy is a human goal. Everyone, seemingly, wants to be happy. This is reinforced by our environment; we read and hear narratives everywhere telling us we should be happy, and that we deserve to be happy. Advertisers constantly use the concept of happiness as the outcome of purchase; "Buy XX and it will make you, your child/partner/relative happier" they tell us. Most of us, at some point in our lives, find a point, a place, where we are happy or at least content with ourselves and our life. For the majority, this was in our youth and, as we reach middle age, it can begin to fade away.

But it does not have to.

In some ways, it's unsurprising that people over the age of fifty, and women in particular, face challenges to their happiness. By the time you reach fifty most women have experienced many ups and downs in life. Each person experiences life differently and challenges may affect us more or less acutely. Bereavement and isolation, divorce (our own or others in the family), possibly another marriage, redundancy, complications with pregnancy and the health of children, the challenges of schooling and exams, as well as caring responsibilities of elderly relatives—these can all affect our happiness. Like many women in mid-life I, too, have experienced sadness, challenges and change; divorce (my parents and then my own), remarriage (for both parents and me too), a miscarriage, a parent with dementia, bereavement, redundancy and more.

Women over fifty also face an enormous challenge by feeling invisible, distanced from others, even feeling irrelevant. I explore this idea later in this book.

What makes us happy in the years after the age of fifty is different from the causes of happiness in younger women. How do women manage the ups and downs of life over fifty alongside the physical and emotional changes that are the result of menopause?

We need to maintain, support and find ways to generate happiness and well-being as we age.

Why is this an issue now? Well, we live longer than previous generations, our health is generally better than that of our parents and grandparents; we can look forward to longer periods of being active and, often, employed. Generally, women are now better educated than previous generations. Many have juggled careers and family, travelled more and had a wider range of experiences than their mothers and grandmothers. Women in their fifties and sixties have different expectations of life now from the generations who preceded them. Divorce, for example, is much more common and socially acceptable than in previous generations. And while divorce rates among younger people have stabilised in the UK and US, they have doubled among adults aged fifty and over in recent years. It is also increasingly socially acceptable not to get married at all.

Many women over fifty have and/or want an active, fulfilling sex life, and there's a greater understanding that women want as much sex as men, but they don't want bad sex. Whereas previous generations rarely discussed sex in mid-life, the current mid-life generation can and should be free to enjoy an active sex life without scrutiny. This is important as the benefits of sex as we age are significant.

With greater employment, often more income and freedom to pursue different leisure interests or education as we age, women in mid-life have more choices. They have the chance to be more entrepreneurial. Using digital technologies and social media, many more women are setting up successful small businesses in their fifties than ever before. The opportunity to sell goods and services online without the need to have physical premises means the set-up costs of a business are much lower and less risky than before. Using social media as well as other promotional campaigns, new businesses can find a wider audience for their services or goods. This is a global phenomenon and just one example of how women in mid-life and making the most of opportunities not available to previous generations. Importantly, such activities provide purpose, a core component of happiness which I will explore further in this book.

Women over fifty now present almost an entirely new social group. By the time they reach fifty, they can generally expect another third or more of their lives to lead. They are generally stronger, more active and healthier than the generation before. They want more, will contribute more and have a huge potential to be happy. But there is no guidebook to making this third part of life happy or even contented. This is, socially, almost unexplored territory. Where our mothers and grandmothers were typically expected to remain married, keep home, help with grandchildren and be satisfied, this new social group of the twenty-first century has the opportunity to do much, much more. I aim, in this book, to offer some thoughts about how to seize these opportunities, navigate the changing landscape and find happiness or at the very least, greater contentment.

I take a look at the issues that affect women's happiness in later life, including health, attitudes towards sex and how sex makes you feel happier and less depressed, the importance of relationships and avoiding loneliness. I explore some of the research that explains the issues that affect happiness and well-being and try to provide some insight and suggestions for a happy life. We all have the capacity to be happy. Understanding what affects our happiness helps us to take steps to live our longer lives more positively.

Some of the factors involved in our happiness: women's stories

I interviewed scores of women as part of my research for this book, and many more freely contributed their thoughts and attitudes towards happiness as we age. I wanted to hear their stories and explore similar experiences and themes. Here are a few examples of their stories, with more in the chapters that follow (names have been changed in all cases). The common thread is that as they hit mid-life, there are serious threats to their happiness and general life satisfaction. Some responded to the challenges. Others have found it more difficult to do so.

Divorce and changes in family life can dramatically affect our happiness and those involved. Abina is a very fit woman and I often see her in my gym. She looks ten years younger than her biological age. She told me that her enviable physique was hard won after the end of an unhappy marriage. "I got to my late forties," she said "and I realised that I wasn't happy and needed to change my life. I wanted to feel differently, be more positive and be a good role model for my daughters."

Another story came from Ruth who told me that she was completely unprepared for the symptoms of menopause that "seemed to come on like a thunderstorm." She started suffering from menopausal symptoms aged forty-eight. "Apart from the hot flushes which were horrid, I had devastating mood swings meaning I was really, really irritable, and I put on weight. I no longer felt like me and the worst thing was that it was difficult to find the right help or somebody to understand what I was going through. Some people suggested that it was all part of being a woman and I was supposed to put up with it."

Another woman, let's call her Selina, told me that she realised something major was happening to her body when she no longer tolerated her husband's family. "It was if something snapped inside me. I decided I could not put up with the way my sister-in-law was behaving. I had passively put up with all the chaos she creates year after year. I am usually quite calm and not easily upset. Overnight in my mid-fifties I became someone I almost didn't recognise. I now know this was the menopause and all the hormone changes involved. I had no idea it would it affect me this way."

Our ageing process is stimulated by hormone decline, specifically oestrogen. The *menopause* is a natural part of ageing that usually occurs between forty-five and fifty-five years of age but the physical changes in our bodies and effects of hormone decline can make women miserable. These include tiredness, increased urinary tract infections, mood swings, and loss of libido. This subject, though becoming more discussed in the media and online than ever before, is not always discussed in families or between friends. For some of us, the menopause is a taboo subject and many more are ill-prepared for the physical and emotional changes that accompany this inevitable part of ageing for women. Media coverage is sometimes confusing, especially concerning hormone replacement therapy (HRT) as a treatment for menopausal symptoms. I will discuss the menopause in greater detail later in this book.

Isabelle, another woman who contributed to the research for this book, told me that her happiness had been badly affected when her youngest child left home. "When the boys (her older children) left home I missed them of course, but it was when my daughter left for a gap year abroad that I really felt the glums descend. My husband said I was mourning her like she was dead. The house was empty, and I missed her so much, she is such a ray of sunshine."

She went on to tell me: "I had to do something and luckily a promotion became available where I work. I was successful—I got the job—and while I still miss the kids, I am much happier with new things to focus on." When children leave home after being the focus of a family over many years, it can result in feelings of loneliness and sadness. The so-called *empty nest syndrome* affects men as well as women and is not universal but very difficult for some.

I met Marina through some mutual friends. She told me that she became severely depressed in her late forties, and this led to a dependency on antidepressants. She sought and was provided with professional help and support leading to an understanding of the causes of her depression. She was lonely and isolated. Marina came to live in London from Norway to work in her early twenties and married quite quickly afterwards. She had a child, but the marriage broke down and she missed the family network that would have provided the support she needed as a single parent. Loneliness and isolation can be the biggest cause of depression as we age.

I recently admired the bright green coat my friend Cathy was wearing on a gloomy November day in London. "I have made the decision to wear clothes that make me stand out a bit more," she told me. "Suddenly I have become invisible, and I don't like it much" she said. Cathy is fifty-two, a successful lawyer, happily married with two teenage daughters and yet she feels that she is unseen. This is a common feeling in mid-age women, and it is not conducive to happiness.

Sound familiar? It seems that there is an invisible epidemic of unhappiness for women in their late forties, fifties and sixties. Over fifty, we can often feel we are invisible or irrelevant. The world is optimised for the young. Social media, entertainment, fashion—all these industries which canvas our worlds with images and videos centre on the younger generations. Social media is dominated by images of glorious youth, and while women are increasingly portrayed in a more positive way in the media, in TV advertisements middle-aged women are still often used as background. They tend to be the lead character only if the ad is for cleaning products or something to do with their gender, like beauty products. Otherwise, they are firmly in the background.

These are just some of the stories I found in researching this book. The problems women face in this period of their lives is often not seen and rarely spoken about. It's time for us to have a frank conversation about what's going on and discuss how to support our well-being in later life.

The mid-life dip in happiness

Our mid-life dip in happiness has been well-researched and consistently shows the relationship between age and life satisfaction as a 'U' shape. We are happiest—women and men alike—in our early twenties. The lowest level of satisfaction occurs in middle age (roughly around forty—fifty-five years, though individuals differ). Happiness dips towards middle age and then rises again over the age of sixty. Why is this? It could be that those parts of life that challenge us most are at their peak in middle age. This pattern is not universal but fairly consistent in countries that have higher than average incomes. In better-off English-speaking countries, the lowest levels of well-being are in the forty-five-to-fifty-four-year group.

Sasha, in her mid-fifties, explained her mid-life gloom: "We're sandwiched between teenagers sitting key exams and elderly parents with increasing health problems. There's angst at every turn." I know many women share her feelings.

News coverage can affect our happiness

Our happiness is also affected by the wider world especially the news coverage of horrific global events and divided opinions between people and nations. Political rhetoric and the views of neighbours and family which are vastly different from our own can all lead to feelings of pessimism. Social media has the capability of amplifying the worst news and the most extreme opinions, with things or ideas that would not normally be said in person. It can be hard to manage our own happiness when you read bitter narratives and hear angry voices, even close to home. Clashing international agendas, job insecurity and the rise of automation has led to what some call an *Age of Insecurity.* It is very important for us as individuals to maintain perspective and not succumb to pessimistic thoughts about things over which we have very little control.

What can we do about our happiness?

Let's begin with a definition of happiness.

Contemporary happiness research is focused on both the outcomes and causes of happiness and it's that research that interests me. Throughout this book, I use the terms happiness and well-being, satisfaction with life, or quality of life interchangeably. Subjective well-being is a common term in behavioural science and psychology that hints that measuring happiness is through self-report; we measure happiness by asking people how they feel, typically examinations of evaluations of happiness and their experiences of happiness.

The definition I am most drawn to from is from the internationally renowned expert on happiness, behaviour and public policy, Professor Paul Dolan, who was Head of the Department of Psychological and Behavioural Science at the London School of Economics while I was a postgraduate student there. Professor Dolan suggests states that happiness can be defined as "experiences of pleasure and purpose over time." What this means is that we experience positive and negative sentiments from day to day, even moment to moment, that are identified as pleasure, pain, pointlessness and purpose. Moments of pleasure, such as having a good meal and spending time with people we love, are the aim alongside feelings of meaning, fulfilment and worthwhileness against negative feelings of pain, suffering and boredom. The OECD (Organisation for Economic Co-operation and Development) defines subjective well-being as including all of the various evaluations, positive and negative, that people make of their lives, and how people react to their experiences.

For some people, aiming for happiness, can feel unsurmountable. They see happiness as a constant state of euphoria. This is not what happiness means in this context. If it helps, let's say that happiness means contentment, or a high level of life satisfaction.

Psychologists, behavioural scientists and philosophers have long been interested in happiness and what affects our well-being. In recent decades interest in happiness has increased sharply and there now is a wide acceptance in society of what happiness is and means to individuals. The annual *World Happiness Report* determines happiness in terms of income, life expectancy, social support, freedom, trust and generosity. Most people would understand these as being important to well-being, but what I hear from friends, colleagues and wider groups of women in mid-life is that being happy is a little more complicated and nuanced.

Are women happier than men?

In thinking about happiness, I was curious to know if there is any difference between the genders. Are women happier than men? The answer from researchers most usually suggests that women experience more negative emotions than men. It has been found, however, that generally, women's more intense positive emotions balance their higher negative feelings. This suggests we experience more ups as well as more downs.

The influence of genetics and environmental circumstances on well-being is significant. The genes we are born with affect our lives in many ways; increasingly we understand that our genetic make-up affects how healthy we will be across our lives, our personality and even our outlook on life. There's also research that shows a person's happiness returns to a set-point, even after a major life change, such as losing one's job or a divorce or even winning lots of money. The concept explored in this idea being that your happiness is broadly set for life within small limits. The idea is much debated but something to think about yourself in your own evaluations.

Taking all things in consideration, rate how happy you feel right now on a score between one and ten, where one is really very miserable and ten is ecstatic.

Then think back. Is this rating typical for you? Perhaps you feel like a six or seven right now. You may have had very unhappy times when you know you would have rated your happiness as more like a score of three or four. And perhaps on the day you got married, had your first child or passed a significant exam your score may have risen to a nine or even a score of ten. The aim here is to help you to maintain a seven and upwards as a constant, allowing for the natural ups and downs.

A variety of environmental or external influences affect happiness, including relationships, community, work, income and personal freedom. If you are out of work and struggling to make ends meet, this is going to affect most people's happiness. And if your relationships are going through the doldrums—fights with siblings, partners, children, or spouses—these difficult times are all going to affect how you feel about life. I explore all these major issues in this book.

If we have experienced problems and circumstances in early life that are not conducive to happiness, it's important to take steps to reinforce happiness in later life. Experiencing divorce in the family when you are young can make children unhappy, similarly illness and bereavement. It is, however, unrealistic to expect life to be joyful all the time. We will all have times of sadness but hopefully these are balanced with times when life is really pleasurable. This book is about the steps or choices you can take to support your well-being and happiness in mid-life. In the chapters that follow I explore some of the evidence that exists for maintaining happiness levels aiming to give practical tips about what to do towards having years of general well-being. Changing what you *do* rather than just what you *think* seems to be the best route to better well-being. We have the capacity to be happier. Our brains are hard-wired for optimism. It may be that in order to survive our ancestors focused on the here and now, hunting for today's meal rather than worrying about being consumed by larger worries that may or may not happen (or huge predators on the horizon). Furthermore, most research indicates that a positive outlook on life is linked to greater achievement in life and better health. The happier you are, the more successful and healthier you are likely to be.

The secret is to find what suits you and it may be very different from the next woman or man. What I know is that you need to focus on your own values, your needs and what's important to you. This is not a one size fits all book, more a consideration of some of the major factors that affect happiness in mid-age women. I have interviewed and spoken with a wide range of women to find out what they think about key issues, the worries they have in mid-age, and explored their outlook for the future. Their experiences and views have influenced my opinions alongside my own experiences and research findings.

Women need to examine what works for each of us—and while there are many common themes and similar issues, it's not the same for everyone—then follow a path to increased happiness.

Chapter 2
Relationships, social interaction, and happiness

We are happiest when we have access to friends and family. Maintaining relationships with others as we get older is one of the key factors in promoting long-term happiness and one of the most important themes of this book.

Our ancestors knew that being part of a group provided practical as well as social and emotional support, improving rates of survival of individuals and children. Psychologists and sociologists have long established the link between well-being and relationships. Humans are social beings, and we instinctively gravitate towards groups and form connections with others.

Why we need other people

When we experience difficult times in life, we know that the support from others, through family networks and friendships, helps. Being able to talk about problems and get opinions, advice and sympathy from other people helps us to manage everyday life. Having friends and family and being sociable plays an important role in protecting us from situations and changes in our life that may cause distress.

Experiencing major changes in life can affect our ability to cope and may also influence the type and number of social interactions we have with other people. Losing friends and contact with people with whom we have had close relationships in the past may result in becoming isolated and this is a concern for adults as we age.

"I divorced in my late forties," one woman told me, "and for a few years was focused on bringing up the kids. He, my former husband, helped but they lived most of the time with me. Then a few years on I realised how lonely I had become as the kids became more independent. I was really sad, and life looked pretty bleak for a while. I would never have predicted that I could be lonely, it sort of crept up on me." Being isolated can lead to loneliness, emptiness and depression and very often adversely affects our health and happiness.

It is important to find new friends as we get older and nurture them—real life friends that you trust, value and want to spend time with.

Your personality type affects the sort of relationships you need to feel happy

Most people are familiar with the idea of personality types and how they influence our behaviour. Personality also affects relationships and well-being. Extraversion or the extraverted type (also called extrovert) is one of the most studied traits in psychology. Knowing whether you are extraverted, or an introvert may help to explain your preferred type of social interaction with others. In its simplest form extraversion reflects the extent to which a person is interested in and enjoys social interaction. Extraverts tend to be energised by social gatherings. Introversion, considered to be the opposite of extraversion, is a stable and often inherited personality dimension characterised by a preference for quiet settings and solitude. This does not mean that introverts are unfriendly, lethargic, or cold; instead, they are better described as reserved and even-paced, more likely to be drained by the type of social situations that are highly stimulating. Think about big gatherings of people all interacting together, this is what introverts can find draining and extroverts stimulating. Note that introverts are not fearful or anxious of social situations, it's simply a preference.

Recent research by psychologists has focused on individuals who are neither strongly extraverted, nor strongly introverted, called "ambiverts." Ambiverts are those people who are characterised by being ambivalent about social situations, sometimes enjoying the company of others, but also enjoying being alone at times. All types need relationships; they just need different types and quantities of interaction with others.

Understanding your own needs is important in determining well-being.

As we get older, we are more vulnerable to losing friends and family

We want to avoid social isolation at any age, but as we get older, we are more vulnerable to losing members of our social networks. There is more risk of losing family members as we get older; inevitably our parents reach the end of their lives, and our children grow up and become more independent. Stressful life events can result in losing networks too, such as through a severe illness. Becoming ill, possibly spending long periods in hospital or convalescing at home can quickly separate us from friends and being sociable with other people. Divorce and separation can also have drastic effects on our social circle. Established family networks are often dramatically changed following relationship breakdown. Lisa talked to me about the friends she considered loyal to both her and her former husband, and how there was a slow migration to "his side" after their divorce became final. "I was quite upset to see how I had been replaced in what was our social group. My ex left me for someone new, and she simply took my place. He carried on socialising with the old crowd with her instead of me. It was really upsetting. I was abandoned by him, and lots of our friends too."

Many people have experienced separation from trusted family networks and friends for the first time during the pandemic. Instructed to isolate at home and to work from home to avoid spreading the disease has meant that many people have experienced loneliness, perhaps for the first time. There is wide acknowledgement that social isolation of older people has a detrimental effect on physical and mental health, and this has been further highlighted during the pandemic. Social isolation and loneliness increase older people's risk of anxiety, depression, heart disease, cognitive function, and even mortality.

The type of relationships we experience as we age can vary, and we learn that close friends can be as beneficial as a close family. When children leave home and become more independent, our family life shrinks and may change dramatically. The caring responsibilities we may have had with children sometimes are replaced by caring for older relatives, so connections with our peers, friends and neighbours often become more important as we age. Having friendships through organised groups as a result of similar interests, such as hobbies or shared causes can provide a route to forming strong bonds. Friends can be an alternative to family, providing emotional support and expressions of care and trust. I can think of at least three childless couples—all in mid or later life—who have replaced immediate family with friends. They are the ones who organise social events and gatherings and provide the support for wider family members and friend networks.

Losing a loved one can lead to extreme loneliness

A close girlfriend revealed to me that after losing her mother (her father died many years previously) she became aware that she no longer experienced touch; she simply had no-one or no occasion to touch anyone.

She is successful in her career, has many good friends and despite having a few long-term relationships she never married and is now living alone in her fifties. Losing her mother's hugs made her feel very lonely and acutely aware that there is no love interest in her life. The death of a loved one can have long-term consequences on health and happiness. By the time we reach our late forties, fifties and sixties most of us will, unfortunately, have experienced bereavement of some kind. Losing a loved one is one of the most painful experiences that most of us will ever have to face. Grief can easily lead to isolation and loneliness especially if the person shared a large part of our life and our daily activities.

Touch is important as it is associated with the release of the hormone oxytocin; hugging and orgasm have the same effect in men and women. Oxytocin is secreted from the pituitary gland and is involved with social recognition and bonding and seems to support feelings of trust between people. When our oxytocin levels are higher, we feel greater relaxation and general psychological stability. Importantly it helps to reduce our stress response and reduces anxiety. Many women will have heard about this hormone in relation to childbirth and breastfeeding. The act of breastfeeding releases oxytocin helping us to bond with new-borns.

Many people use a change in family circumstances such as divorce, losing a parent or loved one to make big changes in their own life; perhaps moving to a new area or even a new country. It's important to make new friends to replace those who are less available or gone. Age UK, the UK charity that supports older people, says that the effects of loneliness and isolation can be as harmful to our health as smoking fifteen cigarettes a day and is more damaging than obesity. Loneliness and bereavement are associated with depression, sleep problems, impaired cognitive health, heightened vascular resistance, hypertension, psychological stress and mental health problems.

Quality is more important than quantity when it comes to relationships

You don't need lots of friends to feel happy, you need a few people who you trust and can talk to. And it's not necessary to see people who matter to you all the time. I have lunch with an old friend on an irregular basis. We met over thirty years ago when we were students and she's now somebody I rarely see, perhaps once a year as we live a long distance apart. As soon as we are together again our conversations pick up from where we left off. We get right into the deep and interesting stuff about ourselves, our work and families. It's rewarding and satisfying, and I know makes us both feel good. As we get older, we may have more time to revive past relationships. Some women have told me that pursuing a career while also being a mum has meant that close friendships became the casualties of limited available time. They found that catching up with a friend was the first thing to go when work and family pressures collided. When children leave home or become less dependent on mum or dad, friendships can be rekindled. This applies to all of us, high-flyers in the workplace or not. Finding old friends from school, university or early employment can be really fulfilling and sometimes easier than finding new friends as we already have a shared history.

What we know instinctively is that having one confidante that we can speak with honestly and openly is more important than having a wide group of loose acquaintances. It's important to note, however, people also gain a sense of well-being from what are sometimes called *weak ties,* those loose relationships with people we may encounter in our daily routine. Think of the people in the café or in shops that you regularly frequent. Living in a big city as I do can be daunting and the sheer number of people you encounter on trains and buses can make you feel alone and insignificant. Strangers rarely acknowledge each other in a big, crowded city, let alone speak to you. For me, chatting to the guys at the coffee stand at the train station in the mornings makes me feel like I belong to the community. The chat is unimportant, it is simple stuff about the weather but it's nice that they remember small details like how you prefer your coffee order or where you have been on holiday. It can be heartening when the people at the supermarket remember you. This is especially important when you first move into a new street or a new area as many people do when children leave or life changes. The interactions we have with other people affect the way we feel about life. Something to think about, perhaps, when you encounter people in shops, markets and cafés. A small smile or a word or two can make you feel better and influence others' well-being too.

Weak ties are not as beneficial to happiness as the strong ties of close friends, but they do help and should be acknowledged as such. Sarah, a woman in the book club I belong to, told me that a large part of her happiness comes from the close friendships she has made with neighbours in her street. In this case the weak ties have become stronger over time. She says that the support she has received from neighbours during her parents' illness (who live hundreds of miles away) helped her to cope and maintain a normal life at home. Sarah says that a core component of her happiness is these friendships.

The best relationships are those that are positive and supportive, so the quality of relationships matter. Unfortunately, not all relationships are loving or supportive. We may have had relationships with family members or friends that have been psychologically abusive or controlling. Often, the offender has no concept of the lasting pain they have inflicted and in some situations the pain was never intended. The trouble is that negative relationships may continue to cause pain whether intended or not. People caught in poor relationships tend to have a negative view of themselves and find life less satisfying and often lack the motivation to change.

Take the example of a friend whose father was critical of her and persistently expressed negative views about her life that made her question her abilities as an effective employee and her choice of career. She eventually proved him wrong and continues to be capable and effective in all her endeavours, but for a long while her father's words still resonated and undermined her confidence. If anyone questioned her choices or decisions, she was transported back to the past hearing her father's criticism. She needed to take steps to deal with the emotional pain and eliminate the control of the negativity. Part of the resolution was an acceptance that while she loved her father on one level, she acknowledged that he had been less than perfect and much of what she was feeling was grief for the father figure she wanted but never had.

This is an important point because those people with a positive relationship in their life (through family or friends) tend to be less affected by everyday problems, have a greater sense of control and feel more independent. Think about the joy you gain from going on a night out with good friends or the memories stored from a fun holiday with family. These feelings support us in the future. People without any positive relationships on the other hand often become ignored, depressed and isolated.

The quality of close relationships is crucial to well-being. A Harvard study showed that at the age of fifty the number of friends and relationships in our life was a better predictor of future health than any other factor including our genetic make-up. This is an important finding, reaffirming the need for positive relationships as we age. It seems that people with larger social networks are likely to suffer from fewer colds than those with lesser numbers of friends even when directly exposed to a rhinovirus (the virus that causes the common cold). We will explore more about the relationship between health and happiness later in the book.

Are relationships more important to women than men?

Most women will say that relationships are central to their everyday activities and experiences. There is good evidence to suggest that relative to men, adult women maintain more same-sex close relationships and report more benefits from friendships with their female relatives and friends. The relation between happiness and relationships seems to be stronger for women than men. We tend to provide more frequent and more effective social support to other people. I see this all the time where I live, it's mostly the women in my street (with some exceptions) who keep in touch with others and provide support to the older people in the area.

In studies of elderly populations, it was found that older married men rely almost entirely on their wives for social support whereas older women say that they receive more social and general support from a wide group of friends and family members.

There's a theory that suggests that women developed more awareness of the quality of relationships because historically they were more involved with the care of young dependent children. In order to protect themselves and their offspring, women had greater need than men for community and support of families and friendship groups. Perhaps our need for relationships is based on our survival instincts.

Men need relationships and social interaction too, but women's happiness is more affected by the quality of relationships than men and our happiness is more determined by the relationships we experience. This is why it is essential for us to pay attention to our social networks and nurture old friendships and develop new ones.

Is social media a good substitute?

Does the contact with others have to be in person? Does interaction via social media also have a benefit? It seems that in the absence of any contact at all, maintaining and forming new relationships through social media will help well-being. This is good news for people who may be isolated due to ill health or location. Being in contact via social media or online video calls has supported many friendships and families during the pandemic, as well as allowing organisations and businesses to function without in-person contact. Social isolation becomes more of an issue for older adults who live in smaller communities and rural areas since being a good distance away from others and living in communities with fewer people means you simply see people much less often and have fewer opportunities for daily interaction with others. The benefits of tech-based interaction increase if the contact mirrors personal interaction, so a telephone call is better than online messaging and a video chat is better than just calling. We benefit most when we can pick up the audio or visual cues in the interaction. What's interesting, is that the wider use of social media for communication has resulted in fewer phone calls. While messaging through social media platforms is very convenient, it's a shame as we miss out on the nuances of the conversation. Ask anyone who has ever misunderstood a text or message or even email because they didn't have all the subtle hints about how the other person is feeling. There can be many unforeseen consequences of not having the full picture. Being able to see the person you are conversing with through video technology helps maintain relationships, however, especially those living a long way from one another.

There is no doubt that it is better for overall well-being to develop relationships with people and have contact, even fleetingly, in person. Having lots of friends on social media who you don't really know and never engage with on a personal basis is no substitute for a few people who you care about and who show genuine interest in your news and what's happening in your life.

Surround yourself with happy people

Studies have found that individuals who associate themselves and have friendships with those who have a happy outlook on life, tend to have a happier demeanour and consequently better life satisfaction. It seems that the effects of one person's happiness can influence another person's mood, and this becomes a chain reaction, multiplying amongst friendship groups. Think about this—you probably prefer spending time with cheerful friends. The closer you are to these people emotionally, the more prolonged the effect of their sunny disposition on your well-being. If you live in close proximity, so you see more of these positive people, and meet them more frequently, the stronger the effect. It is also stronger between individuals of the same sex.

Perhaps find religion or join a choir

People report increased well-being from being religious and this is particularly marked when times are difficult. If you are experiencing difficult times or life trauma it seems that religion has a greater influence on our happiness. The results are the same whatever the religious affiliation or type. If you ask people about religion and their well-being, many say they gain from both the private aspects of their faith and the benefit of the sense of community gained from being with like-minded people with the same values and outlook on life. This may explain in part why going to church to sing hymns together can increase feelings of happiness. You are sharing the social aspect of worship.

Joining a choir is increasing in popularity and for good reason. Being able to sing along with others seems to me a wonderful route to companionship, forming common bonds and experiencing feelings of joy. Perhaps I am impressed by choir behaviour because I cannot sing in tune, and I am in awe of those who can. There's strong evidence that participating in choirs of all types such as rock, folk, gospel and community choirs is beneficial in a number of ways. Singing together as a community activity has the effect of bonding large groups of people and doing so very rapidly. Because singing is universal—all humans seem to sing—it's possible that it evolved to enable unity between people, providing a good way for people with different backgrounds to bond. If you ask members of choirs about choir life, they frequently say the reasons for taking part include a sense of belonging and the close social relationships that are rapidly formed. Moreover, singing has been shown to increase feelings of positive mood which in turn is a motivator for performances. Compared with other hands-on activities such as creative writing or crafts, singers report greater bonding and increased positive mood afterwards.

Take small steps if joining a big group is daunting

By becoming involved in groups that care about the same issues or causes or share hobbies you are interested in will help to form new relationships and friendships. Volunteering is a way to get started. People form strong bonds with those who work towards a common goal, and sport or exercise are good examples. Go to most gyms and watch women bond through a tough workout, or through a Zumba or Pilates class, to see this in action. Watch people share the exhilaration of achieving a five-kilometre Park Run or taking part in running or walking to raise money for charity. People genuinely bond through charity endeavours, and you gain the added benefit of the altruism boost—we will explore this in further in this book.

Taking part in exercise makes us happier!

There are also physical changes taking place when we sing in groups that are similar to exercise. Singing results in the release of endorphins that are known to be associated with social bonding. Endorphins are peptide hormones, chemicals that help with nerve functionality. Endorphins are part of what makes us human—they are involved in the bond between mothers and infants, in romantic relationships and in human touch. They are sometimes referred to as the body's own natural painkillers as they are released in times of stress or pain. Endorphins are also released during intense exercise or physical exertion, such as in rowing, dancing and even laughing, as well as singing. This is, especially evident in social situations such as in groups. They often cause a wave of pleasure which is why exercise—and I include singing here—feels like a release from stress for many people and can put you in a good mood. We will look at the benefits of exercise on life satisfaction in more detail later in the book.

Another benefit results from taking part in group activities that are not defined by age (like running clubs, cooking classes or yoga). These situations provide the opportunity to interact with people older and younger than we are. As we age, we tend to make friendships predominantly with those within the same age group. With advancing age, it is inevitable that people lose wider friendship networks, and it can be difficult to initiate new friends and to belong to new networks. Being in situations where we engage with different types of people in a positive way through common interest is stimulating and beneficial.

Keep working for as long as you can

Work plays a significant role in the social lives of many and as the retirement age for women and men is soon to be raised to sixty-eight in the UK, the opportunity to benefit from work-based relationships can continue for a much longer period. We are united through common purpose, literally working for the same end goal, and the shared experiences of the workplace. We can spend many hours each day with colleagues. It is not surprising that long friendships are formed through being at work together.

The social networks we gain from being employed may disappear as we get older. If we are made redundant or chose to retire earlier than scheduled, we may lose contact with co-workers and miss out on the daily social exchange that working typically involves. Many people I interviewed for one of my post graduate research projects expressed a desire to retire before reaching the official retirement age, saying they planned to travel or pursue hobbies they hadn't the time for while employed. Many of us will empathise with those aims. Early retirement can result in an improvement in well-being and, potentially, also health. On the other hand, early retirement might also be harmful, because some individuals who stop working may lose a core purpose in life and the social activity that most jobs involve. Most people can cite a story about someone who retired and then gave up on life. This is why most enlightened organisations run courses for retirees and those being made redundant, so people can prepare and learn how to prepare for a very different life.

The key to long-term happiness after retirement is find new friends and new relationships with people to replace those that were associated with work. Jobs are also tied up with our identity, meaning we are often defined by what we do at work. Losing the place of work we go to five or so days a week, and the role we played at work, can be a big blow to our identity, and how we feel about ourselves and our well-being. We will explore the idea of purpose and happiness later in the book.

Social relationships give our brains a valuable work-out as we age

At any age social relationships are predictors of happiness, but neurologists have now further established the importance of friendships and social activities as we age. It seems that the rate of memory decline is affected by social connections. A famous study looked at over sixteen thousand people over six years and those with more active social behaviours displayed half the memory decline compared with those people in the group who were more isolated. The link between social interactions and brain health is well-established.

Developmental psychologists have shown that the intellectual development of children is affected by social influences; it is widely known that children need the stimulation of other people to develop properly. We now know that for the brain to stay healthy as we age, we need regular contact with others, so it's equally important in later life too. Quite simply, neurologists say that being in the company of others is like adding vitamins to the brain. If you think about it, we are problem-solving all the time and this is good for us. It's not about solving big problems necessarily, just small things like looking for keys, working out timetables, how much things cost or even train, bus and tube routes. Being sociable is a type of problem-solving. We look at cues from the behaviour of others, we analyse what's being said and at the same time assess their non-verbal behaviour, making snap decisions about how we will react. Think about how quickly you assess someone in the street coming towards you whose behaviour seems erratic or threatening. It seems that being social not only reduces stress but also gives your brain a bit of a work-out too.

Consider your TV habits too. Watching television for more than three hours a day in later life is associated with a decline in verbal memory, according to recent research. The study looked at the TV habits of men and women aged fifty over a six-year period. Those who watched TV for more than three and a half hours a day experienced on average an eight to ten per cent decrease in verbal memory, while those who watched less than three and a half hours of TV per day experienced on average a decrease in verbal memory of around four to five per cent over the same period. The researchers concluded that although watching television may provide educational benefits through watching documentaries, for example, and relaxation benefits as a way of reducing stress, the findings suggest that adults over the age of fifty should try and ensure television viewing is balanced with other activities. Being sociable, talking to others, makes us use our language skills and watching TV doesn't.

Chapter 3
Family life, marriage, divorce, and happiness

Is being married the best way to be happy?

We all want to be loved. Many of us spend our lives in the pursuit of love. Being loved and loving others is, for most people, associated with happiness and marriage is, for many, the ultimate goal. Happiness is not necessarily found within the institution of marriage., There is some evidence that single women without children are as happy, or happier than, those who are married. While married men report being happier than single men, the reverse is true for women, and single women tend to live longer than married women. Marriage is not always the most social of situations and can lead to social isolation, as immediate family take the place of wider networks whereas single people are more likely to participate in social events. This may resonate with some of you who are married—it's easy to give up friends when you get married, and less easy to replace them. As being socially connected is linked to happiness, this may explain why single people report being especially happy. Thankfully society is becoming more accepting of singletons—single women are less stigmatised than just a generation ago.

While relationships are important for happiness, marriage is not always best it seems. In fact, some of us like a little more space as we get older. Divorce rates amongst the over fifties clearly show that many of us are choosing to leave marriages at a time when in previous generations being single was fraught with risk. Recent research indicates that while divorce in the UK and US among younger people has stabilised, the divorce rate for adults aged fifty and over has doubled.

Living together is increasingly common in all age groups. It could be that mid-age people who choose to live together view this as an alternative to marriage, whereas it's more common for younger people to cohabit as a prelude to getting married. It's also possible that younger people are more selective when choosing partners for marriage than perhaps we were in our twenties and early thirties, when getting married was more the norm in coupledom, and there was more social pressure, both implied and explicit, to get married.

What's interesting about being married is that the quality of the marriage affects our happiness more strongly than marital status alone. Meaning that a good marriage has more effect on our happiness than simply being married or not. Happy marriages make you happy. And moreover, the quality of marriage is generally more important to women than men. This seems to be consistent across cultures.

Divorce rates are increasing in the over fifty age group

The divorce rate among adults aged fifty and older doubled between 1990 and 2010. Why is divorce increasing in the over fifty age group? And is it making us happier? Affairs are now more likely in the over fifties according to one American study and these findings are consistent with similar research in the UK. A statistically significant trend towards increased extramarital sex is being driven by people in their fifties and sixties and the results indicate that the majority of people involved have been married for between twenty and thirty years. The US study indicated that people born between 1940 and 1959 report having the highest rates of extramarital sex. It is possible that as this age group was the first to become adult during the sexual revolution, so lived through a period where promiscuity was more common and socially acceptable. This, coupled with long-term marriages, possibly results in infidelity in later life.

Statistics show that remarriages are more likely to end in divorce than are first marriages. There are many reasons for this, including the pressure of managing complex families involving stepchildren, heightened expectations for a better marriage second time-around, and often the wounds from previous relationships that affect our behaviour in the future. If one of the partners in the new relationship experienced being lied to or infidelity in the past for example, this anxiety may influence the new relationship dynamic, leading to distrust and suspicion without justification. Money also causes problems in second marriages especially where one partner has a child, or children, to support or a maintenance agreement from a previous divorce settlement, especially where finances are stretched.

Divorce is much more socially acceptable now and is even a common occurrence in many western countries. The women I spoke to in my research for this book talked to me about choice, saying they felt that remaining in an unhappy marriage was not the only option. Some suggested that women had an obligation to their own happiness and should leave a marriage if it did not work. Many also said that being unhappily married would not only affect them but their children too. There's also the factor of increasing independence as women participate in much greater numbers in the workforce and can support themselves outside marriage and after divorce. Lack of independent income is also a factor in women staying in less-than-ideal marriages and the reason that many women with caring responsibilities are financially much less well-off following divorce. Newspaper headlines tend to highlight divorce in the very wealthy where men get "taken to the cleaners" by the divorce courts and their former spouses. Like many generic perceptions this tends not to be true for most ordinary people. Women more often fare worse financially after divorce, but this is usually the result of not being able to recover their income having given up or limited their employment to raise children. Getting back into the workplace to earn enough to manage independently after a significant absence can be challenging, but not impossible.

Increasing life expectancies also affects divorce rates; the end of a marriage is much less likely to be as a result of one partner dying. Living longer means there is greater risk of divorce as we age.

Coping with an unhappy marriage

As Isha, one newly divorced woman in her fifties said to me: "I could live another thirty years. I want those years to be spent with someone who makes me happy. And the sad realisation is that my husband and I did not make each other happy."

Marriage and long-term relationships are not static, and many factors influence their durability. For some couples getting through tough periods—family problems, redundancy, poor health and other forms of major stress—can lead to sustained happiness together. Some relationship experts suggest that if you can get through conflict or difficult times as a team the marriage is more likely to continue. If, however, you develop contempt for your partner and all their positive qualities are obliterated (even temporarily), breakdown is more likely to follow.

Counselling seems to work for many marriages that are experiencing difficulties. Talking therapies have much better success rates now than in the past based on the idea that a third party can unlock an inflexible mindset by facilitating discussions between couples. Honesty is important to the process; it helps if partners are reminded of the reasons they married in the first place. An effective counsellor can help to stop warring couples seeing each other as opponents instead developing co-operation and team behaviours. Good outcomes seem to depend on each person's willingness to be emotionally vulnerable and to own up to their part of the problems as well as being willing to participate in the process of bringing about positive change.

If your marriage was once happy counselling is worth considering, but timing is important. Outcomes are generally better if you seek counselling when problems first emerge, not after a trial separation.

What are your chances of a successful marriage? An Australian study suggested that having divorced parents, living together before marriage, having children before marriage or in the first year of marriage and marrying young (under twenty-five years of age) all increase the risk of marriage breakdown. The study also found that women who marry young have a greater chance of marriage breakdown than men who marry young. The study suggested that women who have higher levels of education are more at risk from divorce, whereas more highly educated men have, in contrast, a lesser risk of marriage breakdown. Other studies have shown that happy marriages depend more on joint decision-making, honesty and mutual commitment. Husbands and wives often provide strikingly similar responses in research on successful marriages, citing a sense of humour and consensus on matters such as friends, common aims and goals in life.

While some people are no happier following divorce, it does not mean that lasting happiness is not possible. A significant proportion of divorcees happily get remarried and it's likely that as we mature, we have a better idea of what a suitable partner looks like. Or we simply grow up and with experience understand ourselves more, what we want and what we have to offer in a relationship compared with our younger selves. It's worth thinking further if you are in a long-term relationship where you are really unhappy. Does it or do you deserve action? A marriage that had a good start and loving partners deserves saving—or at least taking steps to try to resolve differences. When a marriage is irretrievable (especially when domestic abuse is involved) then the best option is divorce. Women seem to be more adversely affected health-wise when marriages break down than men. Both men and women in troubled relationships are more likely to be depressed but women seem to more at risk from significant health factors as a result of marital breakdown. The main cause for concern is the likelihood of developing metabolic syndrome, a cluster of risk factors including elevated blood pressure, high triglycerides, low levels of HDL (good) cholesterol, abdominal obesity (or fat around the midriff), and elevated blood sugar—all of which can lead to heart attack or diabetes.

Finding new ways to be happy after divorce—the dating challenge.

Dating can be daunting at any age -- and possibly more so for women in mid-life. Many are returning to the dating game after a long absence after marriages and raising children. Everyone I spoke to for this book says how much dating has changed since their last time being single. Dating apps abound. Where once there may have been a glance across a crowded room, there is now swipe right or swipe left.

Most of the women who contributed to this book who were either widowed, separated from partners, or divorced, expressed an interest in dating again. Some women had previously abandoned the idea of a new romantic relationship, despite being single for some time, as they had been distracted by bringing up children—often alone or with little help from former partners. "I just haven't had time to think about meeting a new man", said Olena. "I wouldn't even know if someone found me attractive now. I stopped looking a long time ago. When my husband died, my focus was entirely on the kids". She told me that now her children are older, she wanted someone to share some of her leisure time, and she confessed that a little bit of attention would be nice too. It can be challenging to think about meeting new people when you are out of touch with dating or even flirting. So where do you start?

Firstly, you have to decide *to* start. Don't feel under pressure to date even though it may seem that there is an expectation from friends, family or from society in general. If, and when, you decide to start dating, do so without unrealistic expectations. The next love of your life is unlikely to be one swipe away. Be open to meet new people, be open to new experiences and be prepared to laugh about it all.

In my view, we put too much pressure on ourselves and others to be perfect, when having some fun with somebody compatible would be a good start. Don't stake your happiness on meeting the perfect partner. Meet someone for a coffee during the day, talk and listen (important) and understand that there are other people out there who are equally keen to find companionship or perhaps more. All the usual safety rules apply—meet somewhere public, let others know where you are, and be prepared to walk away if it really is not working for you. Don't put pressure on yourself to make something work but be receptive about meeting new people. You may be pleasantly surprised.

Tell people—those you trust—that you are keen to meet someone new. In my experience friends can be a good source of relationship prospects. Your friends and family know you well so if you are hesitant, their recommendations can be less daunting. Be receptive to invitations and opportunities to socialise as you need to increase the opportunities to meet others wherever possible.

Natasha, a lady in her late fifties, explained that she had enjoyed two long term same-sex relationships, but never married. She found herself single again and, being an active person with lots of friends, she thought that a romantic relationship was not going to happen for her again. She explained that this was fine until she realised it had been nearly 10 years since her last relationship—or even a date. Friends advised her to try dating apps and she did so with enthusiasm, except that she found fault in everyone she met in person. "She needs to be exactly right if I am to start a relationship again—I have been alone for so long. I don't want to compromise." In seeking a perfect new partner, Natasha forgot that she herself is flawed—as we all are. She was advised to hold back the critique and start having fun.

Dating is a minefield for people of most ages, but women in mid-life generally have sufficient experience and, hopefully, good judgement which should, if they have the confidence, enable them to enjoy meeting someone new. Aim to meet new people, to connect, to share stories, to have fun. With that mindset, dating might contribute to your happiness.

Make friends with your children and stepchildren: modern complex families

Rising divorce rates and remarriages result in different types of families where stepchildren and half brothers and sisters are common. I have seen that women in these scenarios can play a vital part in making complex family relationships work, and this also influences individual happiness. I am not suggesting that men do not play an equal part in the happiness of families—of course they do—but this book is about women and how we can be happy. Making friends with your stepchildren and maintaining a good relationship with your own offspring will affect your happiness and that of the people to whom you are close

It is worth thinking about the dynamics that change within families when parents meet someone new. It's understandable if stepchildren are jealous of the time your partner spends with you especially if it means they spend less time alone with Mum or Dad. It can be very challenging to manage unhappy children when they are not your own. If situations get worse, making people choose between relationships is not a viable option and, in my experience, will cause great misery. One woman told me about her sister, insecure in her new relationship with a divorced Dad who had a teen daughter, became fed up with the family drama in which she became involved. She insisted her new husband choose between her as the new wife and his difficult daughter. This was not a road to happiness for any of the three concerned. In this scenario if he chooses the new wife, he will always regret the impact that has on the relationship with his daughter—that he put his daughter second. The daughter will resent the new partner and feel cheated by her father, possibly causing lifelong bitterness.

Divorce is very rarely if ever the fault of the child/children, but they often feel that it is. Providing there is not a good reason to limit access (such as in abusive relationships), is it fair to punish a former partner, stopping them getting access to a child if the relationship breakdown is confined to the adults? I have been a stepchild in three family scenarios (my mother remarried twice, my father once—all between my late teens and early twenties) and the situations that were most conducive to happiness for all concerned were those where the new partners were sympathetic and supportive but not judgemental. My late stepmother, married to my father for over thirty years, was always quietly supportive but never interfering. She hosted an engagement party in her house when I first married and was sympathetic when that marriage rapidly ended. She was enthusiastic about my second wedding and kind to my children. She was undoubtedly a person with a good heart but her wider motivation, I am sure, was that these actions made my father very happy—something I am very grateful for—and his happiness influenced her own. We all won in this scenario.

It's hard to learn about women who allow new relationships with partners and spouses to influence the long-term happiness and well-being of their children. There will always be a period of adjustment for children when parents form new significant relationships. We can help outcomes for ourselves and our families by keeping a dialogue with an ex-spouse and avoiding voicing negative sentiments about new partners in front of children, however wronged you may feel. The most overriding aim for divorced or separated parents must surely be for children to be reassured that they are loved and that the end of the relationship is not their fault. Do this and you will support their happiness and your own well-being.

Do children make you happy?

Ask most parents and they will agree that children are both challenging and the source of tremendous joy. The deep love a parent has for a child is often cited as the most pure and intense emotional human bond. There's a widespread belief in most countries that children bring you happiness. It seems that we embark on parenthood with the dream of beautiful perfect offspring, even when we know that the reality is one of stress and angst alongside the pleasure children can bring. Perhaps we are biologically programmed to have a positive view of child-rearing to maintain the species. Having children does not always mean an ideal happy life. These feelings are not always easy to acknowledge. In studies parents often report significantly lower levels of happiness and marital satisfaction compared to couples without children. This is particularly evident in the early years of child-rearing. Those of us who have been through sleepless nights, feeding problems and general health worries of children in their first years of life will relate to these findings. "I didn't find the first months of motherhood easy. In fact, it was hell at times. It was not what I expected; I wasn't very well and the baby, my daughter, didn't sleep. It was a really tense time between my partner and me—not the happiest of times," one woman told me. "Things got better and by the time I had my second child, three years later, I was more prepared for how challenging children can be in the first two years."

Misgivings about having children are more common in younger adults than in older parents. A YouGov survey from 2021 shows that younger parents aged between twenty-five and thirty-four are the most likely to have regrets with one in five bitterly regretting having children. Those aged fifty-five plus express the least regret with only one I ten being unhappy about their decision to have children.

Overall, the YouGov survey revealed that one in twelve parents (eight per cent) regret having children, while a further six per cent previously had regrets but have changed their minds.

What's interesting for those of us with older children is that there's evidence that the challenges of parenthood are not restricted to the period when children are economically and physically dependent. Older parents whose children have left home report similar or slightly less happiness than couples who have never had children. "Small children bring small problems; big children bring bigger problems," I was told by a mum whose three offspring were all in their early twenties. "You never stop worrying; their relationships, getting the right qualifications, managing money and jobs. With three children there's always one who is having a problem." It's clear that we can't always expect an upsurge of joy later in life. Families face different problems when children are entering adolescence and early adulthood, and parents at the same time are facing their own challenges of mid-life.

"It has been one of the most difficult times for me as a parent," Elodie told me, "I hit the menopause almost at the exact time that my daughter reached peak adolescence. She was anxious and non-communicative, and I was constantly irritable. We clashed a lot and for a while it was hell at home for everyone."

The notion that you are only as happy as your unhappiest child resonates with most parents. We know that life challenges that affect our children will also affect our own happiness. This is not always the case, however. Sometimes miserable parents have happy kids and having happy, well-adjusted kids is not guaranteed to support our happiness. On the other hand, an extremely unhappy or depressed child, while distressing to a parent, may not always destroy a positive parental outlook. People are varied and very different in terms of resilience and outlook, and many factors affect our well-being. As I have already said, your reasons for happiness are not necessarily the same as those of the next woman and we need to find our own way to be happy.

Chapter 4
Health, well-being, and happiness

How we feel day-to-day, from month-to-month, the state of our physical health undoubtedly affects how happy we are. Assuming you do not have a hereditary disease that adversely affects your health as you age, most women (and men) will live a longer life than previous generations. People worldwide are living longer. For the first time in history, most people can expect to live into their sixties and beyond. According to the World Health Organisation, the proportion of the world's population aged over sixty will nearly double from twelve per cent in 2015 to twenty-two per cent in 2050, In 2020 the number of people aged over sixty globally will outnumber children under five years old. This is all great news, a longer life offers the chance to pursue something new, such as learn a new skill, find a new career, and explore a passion or long-neglected hobby. How much we do, for ourselves, for our families or even the wider community will, however, heavily depend on our health.

Look around you and you will see that how we age varies enormously—there's no typical old person. Some people will have a fulfilling, healthy older life, but there are many who will not. We know that some of the variations in health in older people are genetic. We may have inherited genes that make it more likely to develop certain diseases, but the most important influence for the majority of us is where we grew up—our neighbourhoods and communities and our socio-economic status (the specific combination of our education, income and occupation). Women who have grown up being well-fed, living in comparative wealth may remain free of the issues caused by ageing until well into their seventies and eighties. Compare this with women who have had to endure a lifetime of poverty, malnutrition, social deprivation and heavy physical labour. They may experience health problems associated with old age at just forty.

It is widely accepted that happiness is affected by health. That's not to say that people with long-term health conditions or disabilities are not or cannot be happy. What interests me is how we support our happiness as we age and how even in mid-life, we can take steps to improve our health in order to prolong life. Most of us don't just want to live longer; we want to live happy, active, healthy lives, where we can enjoy extra years, not endure old age limited by declining health. The good news is that it's never too late to adopt a healthy lifestyle. Change your lifestyle in middle age and you will experience swift benefits including lower rates of cardiovascular disease and improved longer life. There's information everywhere about what a healthy lifestyle means. For women in mid-life this involves four core principles:

- taking regular exercise
- eating a balanced diet which includes limiting alcohol
- not smoking
- getting enough sleep

Eating for well-being

Obesity is one of our biggest enemies at any age but becomes even more critical as we get older. Postmenopausal women have an increased tendency to put on weight. The reasons seem to be as much due to ageing as to oestrogen decline which causes menopause in women. Lean body mass decreases in both men and women as we age as a result of hormones and because we tend to be less physically active. We sit more and move less. We lose muscle mass as we age so we burn fewer calories both when we rest and when we exercise. This may explain why you may gain weight after menopause with the same exercise regime and diet that previously kept your weight stable.

Menopause (and the associated decline of oestrogen) affects the way fat is distributed in our bodies, making it more likely to put on weight around the middle or abdomen, but weight gain may also result from managing the symptoms of menopause. If you are experiencing night sweats, sleep disturbance and mood swings it may be difficult to stick to a healthy diet and regular exercise. You may simply want to curl up on the sofa with crisps or glass of wine to help boost low mood, and an exercise class may seem less appealing for the same reasons.

Does it matter that we gain a few pounds in mid-life? I read a column by a relatively young journalist (in her early forties) recently who expressed joy at the prospect of middle age. She wrote about the freedom of being able to eat what one liked without the pressure to stay slim and expressed joyful anticipation of being able to waft around in elasticated trousers with mountains of plastic jewellery to detract from an expanding girth. Regrettably, it's just not that simple. It's all a matter of proportion of course but putting on a lot of weight does matter to our general health. Being overweight after menopause increases the likelihood of high blood pressure, coronary heart disease and Type 2 diabetes, also some cancers, gallstones, kidney stones and osteoarthritis. We know that weight loss can reverse many of these complications and can reduce the amount of medication required to manage health conditions and help improve longer life. What's important to understand is that the rules change when you get to mid-life. Exercise on its own will not lead to substantial weight loss. You need to cut calories and take regular exercise to help sustain weight loss and prevent weight gain. Most dieticians suggest cutting back on saturated fat and replacing it with unsaturated fats, reducing salt intake and regularly consuming fish—particularly oily fish. Increasing fibre in the diet and including foods that are rich in calcium and vitamin D to support bone health are highly recommended. The benefit to improving diet and regular exercise is also the change in body composition you will experience, losing weight around the abdomen and preserving muscle mass. You will feel much better and have more energy as a result. Losing a bit of extra weight is likely to boost your self-esteem—all supporting your general well-being.

There's a wealth of knowledge from nutritionists and specialists about choosing appropriate food groups to help with menopausal symptoms. This is worth considering. Very often we fall into poor routines with nutrition, eating on the run, snacking between meals and choosing too many processed and high sugar foods over fresh ingredients. Caffeine, alcohol, processed foods and sugary products have all been shown to exacerbate hot flushes so if you see a pattern emerging it's best to avoid all or try a process of elimination to see what works for you to improve symptoms.

Our nutritional needs change as we age and eating well will support our well-being. Here is a short summary that I hope will stimulate further thought and investigation.

Eat more protein the decline in oestrogen during menopause is linked to decreased muscle mass and bone strength so increasing protein intake can help avoid bone fractures. Meat, fish, dairy products as well as plant-based proteins such as nuts and pulses are the answer. You may also like to add protein powder to smoothies or yogurt or to overnight oats (oats soaked in water or milk with nuts and seeds and stored overnight in the fridge ready for breakfast). The protein collagen available in supplements or in powder form has been shown in studies to help build bone mineral density in menopausal women.

Don't avoid fats as it is an essential part of a healthy diet and your intestine absorbs some vitamins, especially vitamins A, D, E and K when they are taken with a fat source. Deficiencies in these vitamins are connected with a heightened risk of developing some cancers and Type 2 Diabetes. Some studies have shown that eating foods with a high omega three content may also help with menopausal symptoms, but these foods have been shown to be important for overall health (to fight depression, improve eye health, improve risk factors for heart disease and much more) so include in your diet. Foods highest in omega-three fatty acids include oily fish, such as mackerel, salmon and anchovies, and in seeds like flax seeds, chia and hemp seeds.

Eat whole grains diets rich in whole grains help fight the risk of heart disease and cancer. Choose brown rice, whole wheat bread, barley, quinoa and rye.

Avoid highly processed food and anything that says low-fat without checking the label carefully. Very often low-fat foods have disproportionate amounts of sugar added to enhance taste. As a result, you may be consuming unnecessary extra calories.

Exercise and Happiness

Research from many reliable sources shows that exercise is good for one's mental health as well as one's general physical well-being. Physical exercise has been identified as one of the most important factors in healthy ageing. Exercise has been shown to increase pleasure and boost positive mood over time, but it also reduces anxiety and other distressing emotions. Many people experience lower anxiety and have less severe symptoms of depression following exercise. There is some research that shows that regular exercisers are less likely to develop emotional disorders during their lifetime compared with those who never exercise. Exercise helps us to maintain basic physical capabilities and to take part in everyday activities as we age. This has an important effect on our psychological well-being and our overall satisfaction with life. If your physical capabilities decline and start to impact on what you can do every day—such as being able to go for long walks, carry heavy shopping or stand on a chair to reach something in a high cupboard—this has an impact on confidence and can lead to depression.

Choosing the type of exercise is important. Try to find something that you enjoy, otherwise it's difficult to sustain. You simply won't have the motivation to continue, and you are unlikely to attend a regular exercise class if you feel out of your depth and unable to keep up with the pace. Think about trying something fun and motivational if you haven't exercised for a while. It's better to start with something that's inspiring to get your heart going, like a dance class which involves motivating music. Or simply walk—a lot—and at a pace so that you feel out of breath. Do this with a friend and have an agreed goal each week that you can adapt as you improve. Again, this is about what suits you; attempting to emulate another person's training regime may not work. The aim should be to try to find a combination of exercise types that involve aerobic activity alongside resistance training as this helps to improve our physical well-being as well as our mental functioning. Keep in mind that our muscular strength starts to decline after the age of thirty and declines by approximately fifteen to thirty per cent each decade over the age of fifty so including exercise that improves muscle mass and strength is important.

There are four types of exercise that help to support well-being as you age:

Strength-training You can use your own body as a basis for building strength through exercises like leg squats or try weight training (get some advice or direction from an expert) to build muscles and keep your bones strong. Lifting weights to build muscle mass and strengthen bones can make everyday activities such as gardening or carrying bags a bit easier as we age.

Core Strengthening the muscles in your core—the abdomen and the torso—helps to support your back to avoid lower back pain as well as producing a flattened stomach. Strong core muscles help improve posture by stabilising the spine, pelvis and shoulders. They create a solid basis for your limbs. Some say that the core is the body's powerhouse as they make it easier to perform most physical activities. The plank is the ultimate core exercise. Try Yoga and Pilates as both help with the core, strength and will improve your balance too.

Cardio-training Walk at a fast pace for twenty minutes on a regular basis or try running (you may love it), or Zumba, Salsa and ballet classes. It's not too late to try something new. Spin classes (indoor cycling) are a good way to safely build up stamina. Boxing training (yes, really—I started to box in my early fifties) helps to burn calories and work the muscles around the abdomen. The aim here is to get your heart going on a regular basis. Don't be put off by the idea of cardio—regular fast walking is excellent for well-being.

Stretching Exercises that focus on your flexibility and ability to stretch can help with stress as well as improve general well-being. You gain a reduction in muscle tension and better muscular coordination. The increased blood flow that results from stretching supports better circulation overall. You want to avoid poor posture and stiffness which can add years to your appearance as well as limit your range of movement. An additional benefit is increased energy levels. Yoga and Pilates help here too.

I am continually amazed by women who take up exercise regimes in mid-life and become serious athletes despite having done little in the years beforehand. We are often stronger than we think. Sometimes it's simply having the opportunity—time that we didn't have when we were younger—to push our bodies and gain the benefit of becoming very fit. I know a woman in her fifties who has become a champion weightlifter, stimulated by her son's interest in fitness. She is tiny but now very, very strong! I met another woman who has become a marathon runner, only having ever jogged slowly around the local park before her children became less dependent on her.

Being fit not only improves your overall health but gives you an enhanced identity and builds confidence. I write this as someone who has always exercised, to a degree, but with more time in mid-life I have tried different types of exercise that have benefited me. I am far from being ultra-fit, but exercise has become part of my lifestyle and I'm glad of it.

Happiness and your gut

A quick trip down any supermarket aisle and you will find any number of products promising vitality, calm, relaxation and even happiness (*happy tea* for example). Increasing numbers of food products, drink brands and types of eating regimes are making the link between what we eat and our mood. This is more than marketing or sales hype; consumers are hungry for products that support a balanced mind and feeling good. There is increasing evidence of a scientific link between food and mood, what is known as the gut-brain axis, the connection between how you feel and what you eat.

Many of us will know already from personal experience that feelings of anxiety are felt in the stomach. Feelings of *"butterflies in the stomach"* before an exam and expressions like *"I'm sick of this"* and *"my stomach is tied in knots"* after an argument are all well-worn phrases to explain where emotion is felt in the body for good reason. Stomach upsets are one of the most common symptoms of stress and anxiety. Like the brain, the gut is full of nerves and the two are connected. This connection is why parents are advised never to have battles or arguments with children at mealtimes as anxiety causes stomach upsets and, unsurprisingly after conflict, children will refuse to eat. It's never a good idea to have an argument with anyone over a meal if you want to enjoy your food.

There is now intense interest in the role that gut bacteria play in maintaining our general health. A disordered balance in our gut microbes is now thought to be associated with, or even the cause of, medical conditions as varied as inflammatory bowel diseases and even depression. In a study of two large groups of European people, those with depression were found to have an absence of several species of gut bacteria. The researchers can't say if the absence is a cause or the effect of the illness, but they demonstrated that many gut bacteria could make substances that affect nerve cell function, and possibly mood.

Scientists study what is known as the microbiome, a collection of microorganisms such as bacteria which inhabit the body in a symbiotic relationship, and how they seem to play an important role in human health. An imbalance of 'good' microbes compared to 'bad' in the gut can lead to adverse health outcomes such as reduced immune system, weight gain or high cholesterol. A person's gut microbiome with a higher number of different bacterial species is considered a marker of gut health which leads to better well-being.

Nutrition has also entered the world of psychiatry, as a relatively new field of interest. The emphasis is to help patients understand how gut health and diet can positively or negatively affect mood. If someone is prescribed an antidepressant such as selective serotonin reuptake inhibitor (SSRI) for example, the most common side effects are gut-related with many people experiencing temporary diarrhoea, nausea, and gastrointestinal problems. The gut-brain axis offers us a greater understanding of the connection between diet and disease, including depression and anxiety.

What can we do about it?

Recent studies show that eating a healthy balanced diet such as the Mediterranean diet (lots of vegetables, lean meat and fish) and avoiding over-processed foods may help to protect us against depression. It's important to note that a better diet may help but it's only one part of treatment if you're feeling depressed or anxious. You should always seek medical support if you are severely depressed. Food will not be the solution if you are feeling really glum but given the multitude of benefits of a balanced diet full of vegetables, fibre, and fish, it will be worth trying. A few other tips:

• Eat whole foods and avoid packaged or processed foods, which are often high in food additives and preservatives that disrupt the healthy bacteria in the gut

• Instead of vegetable or fruit juice, consider increasing your intake of fresh fruits and vegetables in their natural state. Frozen fruits and vegetables are a good option too

• Include probiotic-rich foods such as plain yogurt without added sugars

• To reduce sugar intake at breakfast, add cinnamon to plain yogurt with berries or other fresh fruit, or make your own muesli with oats, nuts and bran

The good news for those of us who like the occasional glass of wine is that red wine has been linked to greater healthier diversity in the gut. In a large-scale recent study, red wine drinkers were found to have increased gut microbiota diversity (a sign of gut health) compared to non-red wine drinkers. This has an association with lower levels of obesity and 'bad' cholesterol. They found that the gut microbiota of red wine drinkers was more diverse compared to non-red wine drinkers. This was not observed with white wine, beer or the consumption of sprits. Moderate red wine consumption has also been associated with better bone health in post-menopausal women. A word of caution, the beneficial effects of red wine were found in just one glass of wine over two weeks, so it's not a green light for heavy wine consumption.

Other studies found that diet can rapidly change the type and balance of bacteria in your gut. It's important to note that in most cases, the gut microbiome returned to 'baseline' after the studies ended, highlighting that you need to consistently eat a healthy diet to make lasting change to your bacteria. Overall, it seems that a good old-fashioned good-quality diet, rather than short stints of 'dieting', is best for improving and maintaining a healthy gut.

So, avoid smoking, reduce the amount of antibiotics you take and eat the right diet for not only optimum weight but for your happiness and well-being.

Sunlight, fresh air, and happiness

We all know that plants need sunlight to thrive and grow. The same is true for humans. We need sunlight on the skin to stimulate the chemical and metabolic chain reaction that produces Vitamin D. This is not new knowledge. Florence Nightingale, the pioneer of modern nursing, considered sunlight vital to providing a healthy environment for her sick patients during the Crimea War in the mid-1850s believing in the "the purifying and curative effect of the sun's rays". There is a well-documented relationship between low vitamin D levels and poor bone health. The health benefits of sunlight go well beyond vitamin D production, however. Scientists now link lack of sunlight to everything from multiple sclerosis to prostate cancer and our mood. Indeed, getting some sun in the winter months helps to overcome the wintertime blues. If you have ever felt that you suffer from seasonal affective disorder (SAD) in winter it may be helpful to know that scientists have found that light hitting your skin, not just your eyes, helps reverse the condition, so you need to allow light to get to your hands and your face in the winter months.

Unfortunately, many of us are not getting enough sun by being inside too much, wearing sun-blocking creams and lotions all year round or covering our whole bodies with clothing. It seems that artificial light inside an office building or our houses is not enough. We need proper sunlight and being outside even when it's a cloudy day is highly beneficial to our overall well-being, including our sleep cycle. Access to sunlight affects our sleep patterns, our immune systems and our mental health. We need sunlight in order to live a happy and fulfilling life. Research indicates that sunlight even affects our blood pressure by stimulating the production of nitric oxide from the skin. This colourless gas causes the inner blood vessels of muscles to dilate and boost circulation which then reduces blood pressure. The impact of sunlight on our cardiovascular health is not widely discussed. Our blood pressure tends to be higher in the winter months compared with the summer months for most people. Studies indicate that the release of nitric oxide by the skin is essential for anti-ageing too. Poor blood flow and circulation to the skin of the face is responsible for advance signs of ageing including fine lines and wrinkles, poor complexion and even the texture of the skin.

New research suggests that our sun exposure over a lifetime—even before we were born—may shape our risk of developing a range of different illnesses, from depression to diabetes. It is clear; sun exposure improves your health, mood and general well-being.

The challenge is to get that right amount of sunlight and manage or prevent the development of skin cancer. When sun penetrates the deeper layers of the skin mutations in cells may occur resulting in melanomas. The likelihood of developing skin cancer depends on your skin pigment, with Caucasian white skinned women twenty times more likely to develop skin cancer than those with African heritage. Dermatologists advise us to be sensible about sun exposure, to avoid burning at all costs, and to apply sunscreen whatever your skin type, but not so much that we get absolutely no benefit from the sun for our general health. We should not become sun-phobic, so worried about getting skin cancer that every part of our skin is covered, at all times. The alternative may mean wearing sun protective clothing. There is increasing pressure on skincare brands to develop sun protection to prevent us from burning, and the skin from ageing, but also to allow the skin to continue to produce beneficial nitrous oxide.

So, get outside and enjoy the sunshine when you can, especially those of us whose jobs require being inside for much of the year. Getting outside may also encourage us to take exercise. Playing golf, or tennis, or taking the dog for a walk for example will all have a benefit on mood from sunlight and being physically active.

Exposure to nature and mood

There's some evidence that being close to nature, being amongst trees and greenery, improves our mood too. Many people advocate the benefits of the so-called *green gym,* in other words tackling some of the more demanding aspects of gardening. A few hours of digging, weeding and general upkeep of a garden, or volunteering to help maintain a local park, provides exercise, sunlight and a sense of calm according to some studies. Gardening provides me with a welcome sense of peace. It's the combination of something physical, almost meditative in the repetitive tasks, alongside the physical activity and pleasure of seeing something grow that allows my thoughts to settle. It's a welcome part of my week whatever the weather.

Many women spoke to me about the therapeutic benefit of being out in the open, saying that even walking a dog in a park or open space, along a riverbank or close to the sea supports their happiness. One woman I spoke to, recently bereaved, told me that joining a local group of walkers helped manage her grief. She welcomed the unobtrusive low-key community but also being able to walk for long distances without any need to make decisions. She could just appreciate the day as it was at that point, the scenery, the sky and changing surroundings. "It helps my general mood, every time I am outside." she told me.

It has been thought over many centuries that nature has a regenerative and possibly healing effect. Plants, sunlight, and other aspects of nature are often incorporated into healthcare environments such as hospitals to help patients improve health outcomes. The evidence for the benefit of exposure to nature is clear; studies have measured muscle tension, blood pressure, heart rate as well as the emotional state of those after being in natural environments with well-documented positive effects on mental health and behaviour. New studies have also found nature particularly important to the elderly, especially flower gardens and outdoor sitting areas of those in residential care. So, try to incorporate time spent in natural environments to support your happiness and general contentment as you age. This becomes particularly important to those of us living in very urban settings—our everyday environment affects how we feel and our general mood. Studies have found that it's not just access to useable green space that matters, such as a park where you could run or walk through, it is also having green spaces nearby that you can look at also counts in an urban environment. The proportion of green space in a neighbourhood is associated with decreased anxiety, and this applies to where you live and where you work. I

Are you worried about dementia as you age?

Many women told me that they were worried that later life would be affected by dementia—for some a major factor in their feelings about getting old. Dementia is an umbrella term that covers cognitive problems such as memory loss and a decline in problem-solving ability. As my father had Alzheimer's at the end of his life (the most common form of dementia) it is a concern I share with many others. Dementia occurs when brain cells are damaged and those affected have problems with communication and their thinking process that can affect feelings and behaviour. Old age is a common factor in those that are affected by dementia, but we now know that a family history can increase the risk. If there's a genetic link your risk goes up from three per cent (with no family history) to six to twelve per cent, but it varies.

What can you do?

While there's no cure for dementia currently, some studies show you can give yourself some protection and lower your risk by following a healthy diet especially eating whole grains, berries, green leafy vegetables, olive oil, poultry and fish, not smoking, moderating alcohol intake and drinking water. A large-scale US study looked at two hundred thousand people aged sixty-four and assessed their genetic predisposition for dementia alongside lifestyle habits. Ten years later researchers found that people with a high genetic score—meaning they had a strong family history of dementia—lowered their risk of dementia if they also had a high lifestyle score (those with good eating habits, regular exercise and low alcohol intake). So, the advice is the same as outlined before—for a happy and healthier life over fifty eat well and avoid too much sugar or processed food, drink less and exercise more.

Depression and inflammation

Being depressed will undoubtedly affect your happiness, and there is not the space here for a detailed examination of the factors, both physical and emotional that can affect women's mental health as we age. I am interested however, in the research being developed to find a connection between depression and inflammation. It seems that inflammatory changes in the body's immune system cause changes in the way the brain works which can cause feelings of depression. According to the World Health Organisation, depression is the leading cause of disability. The problem, however, is that not everyone responds to medication such as anti-depressants. Some research suggests that as many as seventy per cent of depressed patients do not respond to existing treatments.

Becoming depressed is the result of many factors including genetics, stress and issues that develop in childhood or through poverty. There's growing evidence that inflammation in the body can also increase or give rise to depressive symptoms. If you get a cut on the hand the body's immune system reacts to attack possible bacteria and parasites to prevent these from getting into the bloodstream. The result is the cut becomes inflamed, red, swollen and hot. If the injury becomes more widespread our whole system can become inflamed giving rise to what is called "sickness behaviours" such as fatigue, slow reaction time, sleepiness and loss of appetite. Ideally, we sleep and stay away from others to heal and not to infect or be infected by others. If the inflammatory response continues it can cause havoc in our bodies putting us at risk of depression and other illnesses. That's not to say that everyone who has inflammation of some kind will get depressed, but if you suffer from depression you may like to avoid anything that stimulates your immune response. If you have a condition that is caused by an exaggerated immune disorder, such as arthritis, you should not ignore symptoms of depression.

And get enough sleep. If your sleep is continually disturbed or poor quality your well-being can be negatively affected—your mood, mental alertness and energy levels. Lack of sleep can also be much more serious. It has been associated with the body's ability to regulate normal hormone functioning and can lead to weight gain, higher blood pressure, and may affect the likelihood of developing heart disease and diabetes.

Menopause

It astonishes me that menopause is so poorly understood and the subject of such little open discussion. We need to understand and appreciate that menopause is a natural phase in the life of every woman, yet there still seems to be a stigma around it, even a reluctance to discuss or seek help among some mid-life women who are in perimenopause or menopause transition. Menopause is not the start of a decline in life prospects and is not a signal that the best years are behind you. When women in mid-life experience menopause, they may have thirty or more years of active life ahead of them. We live longer, we are healthier, we are stronger than the generations before us. Menopause is a period of significant physiological change but one which we all face, so understanding the effects of change and how best to manage symptoms will best protect our happiness and general life-satisfaction.

There are several key issues I have learnt through my research.

- Most women—me included—are, or have been, ill-prepared for the onset of menopause.
- Menopause is poorly researched compared to other physiological conditions.
- There is a stigma associated with menopause meaning that some women are embarrassed or even ashamed to discuss the issues and the way their bodies change. Menopause is not sexy. It is seen as a clear sign of ageing. It can be unsettling and confusing.
- Many women do not give menopause the priority it deserves. I know some who won't even discuss it with their GP because they feel doctors probably should be focused on "more important" problems. The information I gleaned through focus group research I conducted while at the London School of Economics about attitudes to menopause revealed a strong sense of guilt about asking a doctor for help.

The way women age is strongly related to hormone decline. We become familiar with the effects of hormones on our bodies and our mood from puberty onwards. The menstrual cycle affects women in varying degrees; some of us are almost incapacitated by premenstrual syndrome and others breeze through adolescence with barely a blemished face or experiencing menstrual cramps. Such is the case in mid-life with the menopause. Research suggests that one third of women experience menopause with little impact on well-being, a third are moderately affected and the final third experiencing often severe and debilitating symptoms.

Like many women I was not prepared for the onset of the menopause. Looking back, I spent a few years sure that various physical symptoms I was experiencing were caused by all sorts of different conditions when I was simply in the perimenopause stage (the years and months leading up to menopause). I thought I knew what to expect, understanding that menopause is the end of menstruation and no longer being able to have children, but I didn't know what else happens to our bodies as women. I was vaguely aware of the key hormones that control the reproductive system, oestrogen and progesterone, but did not know how they affect us as they naturally decline. My best advice to anyone reading this who is in their mid to late forties and not informed, is to find out about menopause. Don't explain your mood swings and physical changes as something else entirely. Many women think that talking about menopause is taboo, almost something to be ashamed of, or as the end of active life and that's not helpful for well-being.

It's worth taking a few minutes to explain what happens. Hormones are the messengers in the body that travel through the blood stream to start, stop, speed up or slow down our physical and chemical functions and processes across all body systems. Your ovaries are the source of oestrogen and progesterone, the two key hormones that control the reproductive system, including the menstrual cycle and fertility in women. During menopause our ovaries stop releasing eggs (many women don't know that we are born with all the eggs we will ever have). The reduced functioning of the ovaries also causes oestrogen levels and other hormones to decline which results in periods slowing down and then stopping. Menopause is a normal, natural process. Perimenopause is the months or years before periods stop. Symptoms can start in perimenopause. The age for the menopause is typically between forty-five and fifty-five with average age in the UK being fifty-one. Usually, most symptoms last for around four years from your last period, but they can last up to twelve years in approximately ten per cent of women.

The physical changes that result from menopause are many. Here's a quick summary:

The **decline in oestrogen** that is part of menopause causes the combination of hormonal and biochemical fluctuations that can lead to changes in your brain and nervous system. Symptoms vary from woman to woman but can include irritability (my primary symptom), fatigue, memory loss, problems focusing, mood swings, night sweats, hot flushes or flashes, stress, anxiety and depression.

Bones and bone loss After the age of thirty, the creation of new bone cannot keep up with the rate of bone loss in your body. Oestrogen depletion results in an increased risk for low bone mineral density, osteopenia (the early signs of bone weakening) and osteoporosis. There is a marked difference between the sexes here. Women will lose up to twenty per cent of bone mineral density in the five to seven years after menopause. Men lose bone density at a continuous but much slower rate in middle age. By the age of sixty-five men and women lose bone density at the same rate. The likelihood of developing osteoporosis depends on many factors; your level of bone density before menopause, your ethnicity (Caucasian women are most at risk) and how fast you lose bone density after menopause.

Bone density loss accelerates into a gradual weakening of bones and can lead to a lot of pain, an increase in the risk of fractures, stooping and other injuries. Choosing a good diet, possibly with calcium and vitamin D supplements (get advice from your doctor) and weight or strength training can help. Taking Hormone Replacement Therapy (HRT) helps by increasing oestrogen levels. For many women this helps to prevent bone loss and can reduce the risk of broken bones.

Vaginal dryness Low oestrogen levels can lead to vaginal dryness, irritation or discomfort. Your vagina can become inflamed as a result of the thinning and shrinking of the tissues, along with a decrease in lubrication. This is known as vaginal atrophy. Sometimes this thinning and dryness can lead to discomfort during sexual activity and make your vagina more vulnerable to infection. To make having sex more pleasurable you should use lubricants bought from a pharmacy or prescribed by your doctor. It makes an enormous difference to your comfort and pleasure, so don't hesitate (see chapter on sex in mid-life). I spent a couple of years in the perimenopause stage insisting that I was suffering from thrush, even visiting a specialist. The discomfort I experienced was due to vaginal atrophy, but I did not know this. I remember being in my local pharmacy explaining my symptoms and being offered vaginal lubricant. I declined! I wish I had been better informed.

Urinary tract infections (UTIs) Oestrogen decline can also cause the lining of your urethra to become drier, thinner and less elastic. This can lead to feeling the need to urinate more often, an increased risk of urinary tract infections and involuntary leaking of urine (incontinence) when coughing, laughing or lifting heavy objects; this is really a case of use it or lose it. I have learned that we should all be doing pelvic floor exercises every day. Both men and women can benefit from doing pelvic floor exercises—they can help stop incontinence, treat prolapse and make sex more pleasurable too. Pelvic floor exercises strengthen the muscles around your bladder, vagina or penis in men and the back passage. Pilates classes can help to focus on the pelvic floor as a way of strengthening your core.

Dry skin Your skin also undergoes changes during menopause. The reduction of oestrogen affects the elasticity and water-holding ability of the skin which leads to dryness, itching and an increase in sagging and wrinkling. Oestrogen appears to help your skin heal more rapidly after wounding so post menopause, we are more susceptible to bruising and other injuries. Your skin is the body's largest and most visible organ, so changes are prominent and ageing skin often contributes to loss of confidence. Abundant daily moisturising helps. Some nutritionists advocate that a balanced diet and a collagen supplement may help too.

Facial ageing If you think that changes in your face are more acute compared with men as you age, recent research has proved this is the case. The first signs of facial ageing are shown between the ages of twenty to thirty years, despite variations in lifestyle and environment. Facial ageing is a cumulative combination of changes in the skin, soft tissue and skeleton of the face. The research, which eliminated all factors of environmental damage in calculations, used 3-D imagery of face shapes and showed that facial shape change is similar in both sexes until around age fifty, when female face ageing was more dramatic, being *twice* that of men. Facial ageing is most dramatic in women in early post-menopause and is shown as a flatter face, sagged soft tissue, deeper lines either side of the nose to the corner of the mouth (so-called nasolabial folds), thinner lips, longer nose and ears and smaller eye area. Your chronological age does not seem to predict how your face will age, but the years since your last period will.

Weight gain: Is weight gain through perimenopause and menopause inevitable? There are many medical studies devoted to this, not least because excessive weight gain is associated with poor health outcomes. It is confusing and much debated—is weight gain due to hormonal changes at menopause, the ageing process generally or lifestyle changes? Menopausal-related weight gain and increased waist circumference have major cardiovascular health implications for older women. It has been shown that in healthy women, weight gain and increased waist circumference during the peri- to post-menopause can be prevented with a long-term lifestyle dietary and physical activity intervention. Again, choosing a good diet and regular exercise really matter. Studies also show that not gaining excessive weight may also help to prevent breast cancer after menopause.

It's unsurprising that given the dominance and desirability of youth in much of western society, that cosmetic surgery procedures are increasing. The Cosmetic Surgery National Data Bank Statistics (2018) of the American Society for Aesthetic Plastic Surgery for 2017 reports one hundred and twenty-three thousand procedures of eyelid surgery in women and twenty-two thousand, three hundred in men, for example. Seeing enhanced images on social media can lead to dissatisfaction in one's appearance and can result in a lack of confidence. Many are critical of those who opt for facelifts as an antidote to ageing but we need to mindful that enhancing your appearance can affect self-esteem and higher self-esteem supports happiness. Wanting to radically change your appearance, however, should be discussed and considered with professional support. Believing that a new nose/jawline/face alone will make you happy is probably misguided.

Managing menopausal symptoms

Hormone replacement therapy (HRT) is used to relieve symptoms of the menopause, replacing hormones that decline as women age. Taking HRT has always been controversial and menopause or the so-called "change" has been poorly researched compared to other physiological conditions. Since the treatment first became available in the UK in 1965 there have been conflicting studies and clinical trials about HRT's effectiveness as a treatment of symptoms and its possible adverse health risks. So why is HRT so controversial? The results of *The Women's Health Initiative* (WHI), a long-term national health study launched in 1993 and published in 2002, resulted in many women ceasing to take oestrogen-based HRT in the UK and many countries worldwide. Since then, the findings of WHI have been re-examined several times, with the conclusion that concerns about HRT are not justified. According to NICE (The National Institute for Health and Care Excellence) HRT is associated with both risks and benefits, like any drug or treatment. NICE states that a consideration of benefits and side effects suggests that HRT is acceptably safe and beneficial enough to justify its use for certain women experiencing severe problems during menopause.

Many women choose alternative natural remedies such as red clover, soy and black cohosh to treat symptoms effectively.

Some women I interviewed for this book revealed a preference for Bioidentical Hormone Replacement Therapy. Bioidentical hormones are man-made hormones derived from plant oestrogens that are chemically identical to those the human body produces. Oestrogen, progesterone, and testosterone are among those most commonly replicated and used in treatment.

See a recognised menopause specialist, attend a menopause clinic or nutritional therapist for advice.

Attitudes to menopause and HRT

Whether or not to take HRT is a complex, personal issue. Reaching the menopause stage of life can be difficult in a society that champions youth and increasingly offers products aimed at anti-ageing and is not always sympathetic to ageing females.

Unlike other aspects of women's health such as menstruation, the menopause has long been a taboo subject, even amongst women, although there are signs that this is changing. Media coverage including debate and information has recently increased in the UK. This, in my view, is because many more women are reaching senior positions in organisations, businesses and in the media, are probably in mid-life themselves and are influential enough to start the debate about something that is affecting their lives. This wider discussion is good for all of us.

Women are influenced by the experiences of menopause in their close family (mothers in particular) and friends. Research shows that we are more positive about HRT *and* its benefits when we have all the facts, but more negative when the arguments are emotionally based. In a small research project conducted recently about how women receive information about HRT, I found that some women feel guilty about taking their doctor's time to discuss symptoms for a condition that is supposed to be a natural and normal process. *"There are many people with much worse problems, and I just feel guilty,"* one of my research subjects told me. *"I feel guilty about going (to the doctor) this afternoon as I know how stretched they are for appointments, but I feel just awful, so unwell."* We should not feel guilty about asking for help when the symptoms of menopause make us feel unwell and unable to function normally.

Many of the women in my study expressed a need or desire to manage their menopause as naturally as possible through exercise and good diet. Many said that taking HRT conflicted with their view that a healthy approach to well-being is better than taking any form of medication. This opinion seems to persist even in those who may be experiencing terrible symptoms and despite new research that concludes that HRT is widely accepted as safe in most cases and, moreover, can be life changing. It's important to make it clear that HRT is not recommended if you have a family history of ovarian or breast cancer, or cancer of the womb, or if you have high blood pressure or a history of blood clots. On the positive side, HRT does have a good impact on symptoms of the menopause, helping alleviate vaginal dryness, mood swings, night sweats and is often prescribed for women who have osteoporosis such is its effect on bone health. Like the contraceptive pill there are many types of HRT hormones with different combinations of oestrogen and progesterone. Your doctor will advise what's right for you if you need help with symptoms. The best strategy is to get advice from experienced and informed medics and reliable sources of information (beware sensational media headlines) and then make up your own mind if HRT is right for you. If you're one of the women who sail through menopause with barely a murmur, consider yourself lucky and don't judge others who may be suffering. If, however, your menopause symptoms are affecting your relationships, home life, your ability to work effectively and your general well-being then HRT may be the solution. Your experience may not be the same as your mother's experience, or your friends. Do what's right for you. When these symptoms can last as long as twelve years you should take steps to support your well-being and happiness in whatever form you can. The good news is that now there's no limit on how long you can take HRT, although most women only take it for a few years after menopause and the onset of symptoms.

A final thought: we shouldn't necessarily view menopause as a period of crisis, or the end of a life previously lived. For some women, ageing and the postmenopausal years can bring freedom, growth, self-awareness, reflection, and a reassessment or rethinking of one's role and the future, even a loosening of previous restrictions and a road towards empowerment.

Chapter 5
Purpose

Do you know women who have real purpose? Those are the women who fight for a cause, champion a charity, lead a group (or a business), love their job and are proud of it, or simply have something worthwhile in their lives that provides meaning and fulfilment.

Purpose is a core component of happiness, of general well-being that even affects our health as we age. The importance of purpose is recognised by psychologists and behavioural scientists and increasingly by other influencers. Oprah Winfrey is a well-known person who talks about having determination to achieve through purpose, or what she also says is a calling, and how it has defined and enhanced her life. Those people who have some purpose in their lives generally report higher well-being. What we know is that finding a purpose can take some time. For some, knowing what they want to achieve is identified very early in life. I have worked with young people training to be professional dancers in classical ballet and contemporary dance, a career that requires tremendous determination as well as skill and talent. They nearly all say that they knew that was their goal early in life, sometimes as young as six years old.

For many more of us finding purpose is achieved in our twenties as we settle into a career or find a passion in life, but it is never too late to find something that provides fulfilment. The challenge for some women in mid-life is that they have never pursued a career for a long period, possibly choosing to care for children, support a spouse's career and increasingly having to care for older relatives. While raising a family brings much purpose to life, the change in life expectancy and an advanced retirement age means that women can feel at a loss in their late forties and into their fifties which often coincides with children gaining independence. In the 1960s our mothers had different expectations. The woman's role was much more defined and there were fewer alternatives to that of a mother/housewife and many early careers were interrupted or halted indefinitely for family reasons. Now life is very different for most women. With thirty plus years ahead, how do women in mid-life find greater purpose? Having something that gives us meaning and an identity can make an enormous difference to happiness as we age.

For men purpose is typically linked to a job or career and having a sense of purpose through work is usually related to higher engagement in the workplace and commitment to the tasks involved. Most men get their identity through what they do for a living. Ask a man in mid-life about himself and he will typically mention his job, profession or how he makes a living before saying anything else. Ask a woman about her herself in mid-life and she will typically mention family first, then job or career or hobbies and other parts of her world. Research into work-life balance of women and men in their early fifties showed that women spoke about juggling many roles in life (even if there were no children at home). Men on the other hand were much more focused on either work to live or a live to work strategy—about controlling their work for their own well-being.

Increasing numbers of women in their fifties have fulfilling careers and jobs that they enjoy that provide boosts to self-esteem as well as providing income to pay the bills. While work sometimes gets a bad reputation it can be the source of great happiness for both men and women. This is certainly the case for much of my life.

I am a great believer that women need something that is theirs, a purpose or role that is quite separate from being a partner, wife, mother, daughter, grandmother, sister or carer. These family-based roles provide fulfilment of their own too—it can be satisfying and often feels good to support a family member or godchildren, and to be needed. What I have observed is that when family members stop needing us, or conversely, when their demands become overwhelming, life can feel less fulfilling. Some women feel quite empty in mid-life. You need a plan or a strategy to give you purpose, to allow you to highlight or pursue new skills, your talents, and realise your potential. It doesn't have to be through the pursuit of a big job or major career path. And it doesn't have to be through something critical or life-defining, it's about finding a role or pursuit that provides reinforcement that you *matter*, or that provides a new or enhanced sense of identity. Purpose can be found through education, or training, by being part of a voluntary group where you are working together with others for some common good, by starting a new business in an area you have a passion for and believe in, through a new job or better job where your skills are valued, through being a local activist (perhaps you care about an issue in your area and want to get into local politics), or even being responsible for a local community activity or premises where others look to you for leadership or guidance. Or perhaps by writing a book. The possibilities are individual and endless.

I know a woman who has found her purpose through training for a triathlon. Let's call her Alison. She told me that she has reached a settled path on all key aspects of her life; she said her children were growing up and doing fine. Her marriage, she told me, was like most marriages—"Up and down with the challenges of life, but a good marriage." Alison has a job that she likes and is content with—it fits in with the other aspects of being a wife and mum. Always a runner and interested in fitness, she said that being introduced to a more demanding competitive sport ignited a new purpose. "What makes you drive yourself to train so relentlessly?" I asked her. She told me that there is something within her that motivates her to train with such vigour, and it has resulted in new fulfilment. Alison discovered what she calls inner grit, and being able to push her body, and compete against other women in her age category has really made her happy. "While it's tough on a cold wet morning to get up and run, and missing out on parties before a race makes me question my sanity, the deep satisfaction of beating my previous time is really great!"

Alison continued: "It wasn't that something was missing as such—I was content—but my driven-personality type needs more to work towards, to aim for." A new purpose.

She knows what makes her happy. Training for a triathlon would not suit me and I am sure lots of other women may shy away from extreme fitness, but she understands that her happiness is individual.

Having a goal like training for a race can support your happiness. Through the pursuit of goals people take charge of their own lives and personal goals can have important consequences for our happiness. Life goals may be something you thought about years ago but had not been relevant until recently. We can all remember the major life goals from the teen years onwards. Deciding to train for a job or career path, whether or not go to college or university. Deciding to get married, or not. Deciding to have children, or not. We don't usually associate life goals with mid-life. The big decisions seem to have been made a long time ago. And before you know it, twenty to thirty years have passed and you're caught up in the everyday, very often driven by the needs of others and their goals, by the seasons, by the school and university terms and the only goal we ever have is to go somewhere different on holiday next year. Or perhaps paint the bathroom or clear out the cupboard under the stairs (insert shed/garage/spare room to suit your circumstances). When we are young goals are a core part of growing up and making the transition into adulthood. They come at us thick and fast. We make decisions about what to study, where to live, how we want to earn a living or the passion we wish to follow and who to spend our time or lives with.

There's nothing wrong with any of the everyday decisions that punctuate our lives. Sometimes a relatively small decision can bring enormous pleasure. Deciding to have a dog or other pet is one example. I say relatively small because I know that taking on the responsibility of caring for pets needs careful thought but is associated with great happiness.

Mid-life can be a really good time to reassess our personal goals in the light of current circumstances. You may have achieved all your early life goals and are ready for some more. Perhaps the time is right to think differently and be a little more concerned about your own well-being. I know a lot of women are so used to putting others' needs first that this can be hard. We can almost feel guilty for spending time on our own development.

"If I go back to work who will manage the mountain of washing in my house?" a seemingly intelligent mother of four lamented to me a few years ago. She later admitted that the multitude of household tasks got in the way of her own purpose. There was safety in the routine of the everyday, working and being occupied to satisfy the needs of the home and the family.

In fact, she was fearful of doing something where she may be tested or assessed. She was afraid to start again but she found her purpose through volunteering, starting slowly and building up her time and responsibilities. This gave her confidence that her excellent organisational and interpersonal skills were valuable outside the home.

Education, skills, and training

Returning to education in mid-life can provide renewed purpose. Later life learning is becoming increasingly popular in the UK. The need for adults to retrain or upskill is being recognised by the UK Government who, during the pandemic, announced funding for new skills training to enable adults to gain new qualifications and access new job opportunities. This is very positive in my view, the opportunity to gain new skills or qualification can provide the channel for a different job or new career. And if the training is for a new or developing job sector, the likelihood of employment increases. For some people, gaining the qualifications they missed out on at school, or the chance to study for a first or second degree, is part of a major life transition. Others become interested in education for its intrinsic interest, with no immediate goal other than the education and stimulation it offers. In many ways, returning to education is easier when children are less dependent on parents. Not having to juggle childcare with studying and attending lectures may make mature women especially motivated to start a new course. With opportunities for remote learning and part-time study it is now much easier to train and study.

The main reasons that older women return to education are for self-development, to supplement or boost income, but also to escape loneliness and build self-esteem. My own decision to return to university to study for a master's degree was partly the fulfilment of a long-held goal and partly to increase my skills to boost my career opportunities. I was also motivated by my son's chance to study at the University of Cambridge as an undergraduate. Seeing him become a passionate student, surrounded by very smart people was enormously pleasing, knowing that this is the type of environment where he would thrive. His life satisfaction stimulated my dream of studying for a second degree. This late life studying experience was life-enhancing and a great source of happiness for me. I gained an enormous boost to my self-esteem by being accepted at LSE and, despite the challenges of studying and continuing to fulfil a client project I had started the year before, I continued to find real self-fulfilment throughout the twelve months of the course. This boost in mood was so evident that my husband suggested that I carried on studying as, in his opinion, this was the happiest I had seemed in some years. One study suggests that almost a third of women express thoughts about missing out on opportunities earlier in life, particularly career opportunities. That resonated with me. It is never too late in my opinion to study for the first time or to return to education, particularly as student loans are available in the UK up to the age of sixty* (at the time of writing).

You need to be honest and clear about the goal and outcomes of studying in mid-life, however. If it's a new job or change in career direction you want, then do your research. It makes sense to train or upskill in a sector where there are jobs available. There are many companies and organisations that value older workers and increasingly large companies run programmes for women returning to work, not just after having children but after longer periods of being absent from formal employment. Working in healthcare is one sector that supports retraining and where there are always a variety of jobs available for those with the right skills. Teaching is another profession that is increasingly attractive to men and women in mid-life. A quick search on the internet and you will find a plethora of articles about which careers are best for women over fifty to help the thinking process.

A friend of mine, Linda, trained as a nurse after leaving school and left the job to raise three children. There was a particular period in her early fifties that stimulated a return to her former career: "The children had all left home to work or complete their studies, so I bought a dog, and then I redecorated the house. Then there was a short time when I looked after my ageing Dad who sadly died. And then I woke up one day and wondered what on earth I was going to do now," she told me. "So, I went back to nursing on a *return to nursing scheme*." Linda updated her skills and became a practice nurse in a local GP surgery and says it has made a big difference to her life, not only to her own happiness and self-esteem, but to how others view her. She says that even working part-time has given her new status and restored confidence in her abilities.

Another woman I met has chosen to become an accredited psychological counsellor. This is a completely new area of interest for her and nothing like any job she has done previously. After an ugly divorce studying has provided new direction, a distraction from the arguments and many new friends. Being back in the classroom also adds the opportunity of networking. It is estimated that as many as fifty per cent of jobs are gained through contacts or recommendations so make the most of the people you meet if you decide to study or retrain.

If, however, you want to pursue an interest or passion without the need to generate income then studying, training or learning a new skill has a very different, but also highly worthwhile purpose and can also boost well-being. I know that learning a new language works for some, especially when there's a foreign trip as an added goal. Perhaps you want to study interior design or pursue something in the arts that you have always loved but have never had the time or opportunity to explore. I know women who have, with more time available in their later years, decided to gain specific creative skills for pleasure and interest and have eventually started jewellery businesses, offered painting commissions and knitting/textile design services—all of which are run from home. Others have trained as beauticians, and one has decided to run a vintage clothing business from home.

The other benefit, studies have shown, is the improvement in general physical and mental health for returning women students aged over fifty. In a recent study, student groups in mid-life reported better health, fewer and less severe depressive symptoms and greater independence and self-sufficiency than before commencing their studies. My mother has often related her story that illustrates this point well. As my brother and I were growing up and becoming less dependent on her she found a plethora of reasons to visit her GP with mystery symptoms and possible illnesses (and this is long before access to the internet to stimulate anguish by scouring medical websites). The GP was insightful and suggested that what my mother needed was an outside interest, something to really engage her. What she needed, he suggested, was a job. She says that after becoming a laboratory assistant in a local senior school the mystery illnesses disappeared overnight. She was fulfilled and went on to train to become a biology teacher.

Starting a business

Digital technology is a real enabler for women worldwide, allowing women to run small businesses from home and to gain access to new markets without the cost of premises. So-called Home-Entrepreneurship is booming with women in their fifties.

In 2017 Barclays Bank reported a sixty-seven per cent increase in women over fifty-five opening business accounts in the previous ten years, and for those aged sixty-five and older the number was up by one hundred and thirty-two per cent. As many as twenty per cent of all new businesses are started by women in their fifties. Start-ups are not just for the young it seems. Mature women are particularly successful at starting new businesses, however small, using the skills we have gained through bringing up children, caring for elderly relatives and running homes, often combined with jobs to help pay the bills. A multi-skilled and agile approach contributes to success in mature entrepreneurs—especially where women are concerned.

A recent study (from 2018) found that the most successful new entrepreneurs, both men and women, tend to be those in mid-life. The researchers compiled a list of two million seven hundred thousand company founders in the US with at least one employee between 2007 and 2014. What is notable about the findings is those who started companies in the technology sector. We often think that the tech. sector is populated by young entrepreneurs, however this study showed that the average age of start-up founders of the most successful tech companies was in fact forty-five years. It seems that a fifty-year-old entrepreneur is almost twice as likely to start an extremely successful company as a thirty-year-old. There are many reasons why maturity wins, but one key factor is the difference between ideas and execution; many people have great ideas, but the challenge is executing them effectively. Having the experience (which you don't typically have when you are young) and knowing what works makes the difference.

This is really encouraging for women in mid-life who want to be entrepreneurs. It seems that there is not a magical or intangible factor that drives success, it's a combination of ideas, drive, skills, talent and creativity and know-how that really works. If you are in your fifties or sixties or older and you have a brilliant idea or can see a gap in your market, it's really worth considering starting your own business—it will really give you purpose!

Work and happiness

Older women are increasingly seen as attractive employees. They are adaptable, resourceful and bring life experience and emotional maturity. This is good news as there is often a financial motivation involved in finding new types of employment as we age. It's easy to see why. Living longer and delayed retirement has resulted in a growing number of older workers, most of whom need to work to maintain a lifestyle or simply pay the everyday bills.

There's an added benefit of work—a haven from domesticity. Research has shown increasing similarities in the way in which men and women regard work and home life. In the past, the home was seen as a haven from which (male) workers could escape from the drudgery and stressful world of paid work to relax and be appreciated by wife/partners and family. Now, both men and women report that they regard home as an additional place of work—think unwashed dishes, unresolved quarrels, troubled teenagers, young adults back at home after study because they can't afford rents—so going to work is often seen as a haven. The pandemic, with the need to work from home, and support the education of children at home, has especially highlighted the joy of being in a place of work for some people. "Work is where I am the other me", Mia, a mid-aged woman who works as a manager in exhibitions and events told me: "I love being part of a team. We're all working towards a goal, and while it can be very stressful at times, I forget any troubles or problems at home and focus on doing a great job. That's what I am known for and it's really important to me. I love my family too, but work provides an important balance in my life."

It's worth noting that work-life balance is still an issue for women in mid-life—often affecting happiness—and not an issue confined to mothers with young children. Lack of work-life balance is a problem for men as well as women, and for the parents of older, as well as preschool, children. Women can often feel the burden of juggling paid work, adult children and ageing parents. Research that looked at gender and work-life balance among both mid-age men and women found that women tend to take on the demands and difficulties of home and work for much longer, which often becomes more complicated with changing family dynamics.

Age discrimination is a fact in many companies and organisations and starting a new business from home is a positive alternative. Figures from the UK's Office of National Statistics (ONS) in 2018 show that for the first time there are more than ten million people aged over fifty in employment, a third of the workforce in the UK and equivalent to the population of Sweden. This figure is rising; ONS figures show that just over seventy per cent of fifty- to sixty-four-year-olds are now working compared with fifty-six per cent in the early 1990s. What is important here is that being employed, even part-time, as we get older not only helps pay bills and provide for the extras that give pleasure, funding hobbies and interests, but also gives purpose. Involuntary unemployment is not a route to happiness. Being a valuable part of the workforce, contributing skills and experience to organisations, is.

There's good evidence that working improves self-esteem in

mid-life women. Those who continue to work or find employment over forty-five have been shown to have less psychological anxiety, report better physical health and say they feel better about themselves compared with those women who stay at home. Findings from research also suggest that work may act as a stabilising force for women during critical periods throughout the life cycle.

The important factor here seems to be about feeling valued. If you are valued as an employee for your capabilities and what you contribute to an organisation you will have a stronger sense of self—your identity is supported by your skills and abilities and achievements, even if the achievements are those of the organisation as a whole and not just yours as an individual.

Adriana is in her early sixties and although had a promising career involving her considerable language skills in her twenties, gave up work to raise three boys and support her husband's demanding career. She has always been involved in voluntary work and has studied broadly for pleasure and stimulation. Adriana told me that she had recently been asked to teach Spanish lessons to retirees in her community and that there was a small remuneration for her services. Not only was this hugely rewarding, she also said it made her feel important. In Adriana's situation being valued through paid employment provided personal validation and support to her self-esteem. It's never too late to start working again. The wider value of paid employment has been shown in a US based study with evidence that participation in the labour force may prevent late-life memory decline in women as well as mental stimulation and financial and social benefits.

I am deliberately positive about the benefits of employment—of all kinds—but it is important to acknowledge the challenges of applying for jobs after the age of fifty, for both men and women. The Centre for Ageing Better recently published a report stating "Ageism remains pervasive; older workers are widely perceived to be unproductive, set in their ways and unable to adapt to change. They are routinely overlooked for training and career advancement opportunities." Age and gender discrimination exists meaning that women can find it hard to find new jobs in some sectors. If women leave employment due to caring responsibilities after the age of fifty, they are much less likely to find a new job afterwards. Persistence is key. Use contacts to help you get a job or new position. This means telling people in your network that you are looking for a job. A personal recommendation can overcome bias. If you are a returner in work terms, be prepared to try something new. It's important to highlight transferable skills in any application or interview. You may just have the life experience that an employer needs, but you need to overtly explain your suitability for a role. This is not the time to hold back.

Give back—why altruism makes you happy

Have you ever picked up a dropped glove on the street, handed it to the grateful owner and felt good about your small act of kindness? Have you ever thought that a gift given to a friend or relative, however small, has provided you with equal pleasure as the person who was the recipient? Is it that some people are inherently more giving in nature independent of income or privilege? The fact is that most of us gain positive feelings such as contentment and pride following acts of altruism or even small acts of helping or kindness.

There is a strong link between the well-being, happiness and health of people who are emotionally and behaviourally compassionate. Being helpful to others also seems to be linked to a longer life.

There is overwhelming research to suggest that in helping others we help ourselves. And what's particularly interesting is that the evidence shows the benefits across all age groups, and that altruism even helps with recovery from alcoholism, addiction and depression.

Many people find that formal volunteering provides community, social connections and the satisfaction of supporting a cause or others who need help. Volunteering can also provide purpose—you get the benefit of altruism and a goal—both supporting well-being.

Behaviours like these are not confined to our personal lives. *Doing well by doing good* is the mantra of many organisations who believe that they can gain advantage or social acceptance by including charitable initiatives as part of business practice. Some would say that being charitable is a necessary requirement of modern business, but there is good evidence that voluntary work leads to employee satisfaction. Increasingly we want the companies and organisations we work for to do something more than make profits for shareholders. We also want to feel pride in the products or services we work hard to provide to customers or consumers. Many companies and organisations include a volunteering day of choice as part of their charitable support initiatives. Working together with colleagues for a joint initiative outside the main job we're employed to do supports how we feel about the company or organisation and helps to us to feel better about ourselves.

There's one caveat however, helping others does not make us happy if we are overwhelmed by the tasks or put upon by others. I know a young grandmother who is always happy to help with the grandchildren, but because of her kind and never-complaining nature, also gets asked by friends and neighbours to help out too. She is so used to helping others that she no longer has time to enjoy her grandchildren and the result is a broad resentment towards all.

A final thought on purpose

Having a sense of purpose promotes higher self-esteem, self-acceptance and optimism, but it also been linked to physical well-being and health. This is important for women; studies have shown that higher purpose in life predicts lower hip-waist ratios in older women (the more dangerous weight around the middle) and higher levels of so-called "good" cholesterol. There's even some suggestion that it may be associated with lower risk of Alzheimer Disease and a greater sense of purpose is also associated with more enjoyment of sexual activities in mid-life women.

Chapter 6
Sex, attraction, and confidence

I believe in a healthy and active sex life. It is important to me and my relationship. My happiness is undoubtedly supported by regular sexual activity with my husband. In my view, it is important to be open about sex in mid-life and not, in any circumstances, allow it to become a subject we cannot discuss through embarrassment or lack of knowledge.

An active sex life is associated with a better quality of life and fewer instances of depression. This is fact. Sex is important to relationships and important to our well-being too. It can be fun, even as we get older. This is not just for young couples, married or otherwise, this applies equally if not more so to women in mid-life.

Through my discussions and interviews with women in their late forties, fifties and sixties, I have a better understanding that some of us are simply not interested in sex. Maybe we were never interested, or it is a part of our lives that we have visited, sampled, and then rejected or passed through to choose abstinence, or even becoming in some way asexual. That is fine too. Especially if you are single. Sex is a basic instinct, and most people get enjoyment at some stage in their lives from some kind of sexual contact. Typically, marriage and long-term relationships are bound by certain (sometimes unspoken) rules and expectations and usually they include sex as part of intimacy. If you or your partner change the rules, choosing not to engage in sex or actively abstain, you need to think about what the consequences are for happiness (your happiness and your partner's too) and the relationship itself.

In the past we married or cohabited with little thought about long-term emotional well-being. We married for many reasons: perhaps love, companionship, for security, for procreation and even for survival. If the relationship faltered, we tended to be stuck until one or the other passed away. Women were not always the winners or the happiest in this scenario. Now our expectations are different. These expectations seem to be driven by what we read in books, see in the movies or online. Our idea of a perfect marriage is rarely realistic. We expect that sex should be the same as when we first started making love, full of passion and heady desire. I am mindful of the trope that if you put a penny in a jar each time you have sex in the first year of marriage or a relationship, and then take a penny out for every time you have sex afterwards, that you will rarely if ever empty the jar. Sex is rarely as frequent between couples after many years together, regardless of age, compared with the first phase of a relationship. If the sexual side of a relationship starts to decline after two, three or five years, how do you keep passion alive after ten, fifteen or even twenty years of marriage? And does it matter? It is not unusual for sex to disappear almost entirely from a marriages or log-term relationships. This is what is described as the transition from passionate to companionate love and a normal evolution of a relationship.

It is up to each individual to choose how important sex is to them and their partner. I am an advocate for sex, as it does affect relationships. It is important to explore and understand what the implications of good sex or no sex are for you and your partner, and being able to communicate this can be of benefit to both of you.

Based on large-scale surveys researchers have found an association between sexual activity and satisfaction *and* emotional well-being. There's also a link between sexual gratification and partner satisfaction and how we feel generally about our overall quality of life. Women with more active and satisfying sex lives consistently report better emotional and relationship satisfaction. There's also a study that shows that the benefits can be two-way. Sexual interaction between couples and physical affection improve mood and reduce stress. Improved mood and reduced stress in turn increases the likelihood of future sex and physical affection. In other words, a kiss and a cuddle one day may lead to sex another day. Most women will identify with this idea. We typically want the emotional and supportive side of a relationship as a basis for good sex. We are less inclined if sex is the only way we have physical intimacy.

That women in their fifties, sixties, seventies and beyond are still interested in sex is a fairly new idea. There has been a common misconception that people stop engaging in any sexual activity with increasing age—almost becoming asexual. A UK survey by the English Longitude Institute for Ageing tells a different story. Over half of women over sixty report being sexually active, fifty-nine point nine per cent. In those aged sixty to sixty-nine it is thirty-four point three per cent. In those aged seventy to seventy-nine years it is fourteen point two per cent and under ten per cent in those aged eighty plus. Figures for men are similar but slightly higher in each age group. Perhaps we all knew this as individuals, but it wasn't acknowledged or widely researched.

There are a many psychotherapists and other health professionals who now offer good advice and strategies to help couples get back in the habit of regular sex. I highlight here some of the key issues to make you think and possibly act upon to support happiness. I generally believe that sex is good thing for relationships. To be clear, if you choose to abstain this is your very personal decision that needs discussion and openness with your partner.

Sex makes you happier and healthier

Does this mean you need to be having sex at the same rate as in your twenties and thirties? Not necessarily. We need to be mindful of the benefits of regular sex which have been compared to taking regular exercise. Research has shown that continuing to have sex as we age reduces your risk of depression, making you feel happier and more relaxed.

Reductions in sexual activity have in contrast been shown to be associated with a greater risk of stroke, cancer, coronary heart disease and general ill health. There are also studies that have shown that an active sex life as we age can affect the rate of cognitive decline—helping to slow decline too. What this also means that the onset of sexual problems may indicate ill health or declining health. Something to think about in ourselves and our partners. If you always enjoyed regular sex in your relationship and one of you is unexpectedly no longer interested, it is worth investigating or at least talking about.

The benefits of sex as we age include some protection against heart disease; it supports our immune system and prevents incontinence (see chapter on health and the pelvic floor). It decreases feelings of loneliness and isolation and keeps you flexible and more mobile. It's conclusive—- sex improves overall health.

Some say sex makes you look younger too. Sex certainly enhances your self-esteem and how we feel about ourselves.

Make time for your partner in the bedroom and the relationship will benefit. You will feel more connected both physically and emotionally. Your overall health contributes to our sex lives. If you are healthy, you are more likely to want sex and having sex makes you feel better. It's a reinforcing behaviour cycle.

And just in case we forget, sex can be fun. Although women's sexual peak tends to occur in their thirties, women are capable of having as powerful and rewarding orgasms in mid-life.

Not enough sex and lack of libido?

It's the most common problem for long-term couples. Many of us in mid-life have been married or in a committed relationship for more than twenty years. Sex by this time may be little more than functional and irregular "Birthdays, anniversaries, Christmas and New Year of course, but that's about it. Oh, perhaps on holiday." said one woman to me who is married with kids in the teens and early twenties.

We can easily get out of the habit of sex if you are married or in a regular relationship. We get tied up with the minutiae of life, the small things that take our attention and time. Throw in a couple of kids, perhaps caring responsibilities for older relatives and busy working lives and soon we're tired, lacking in time and motivation too. It's not surprising that by the time we get to mid-life that we have almost forgotten the passion that united us in the first place. Not having sex can affect communication between partners. "If we don't have sex on a regular basis, I know our general communication will break down," Jenna, a woman in her late fifties told me in an interview. "It's difficult to explain. We have sex and then we connect again. But if we don't, say we miss it for a few weeks, then we start niggling at one another.

Kitty said something similar: "If we miss sex for a few weeks, we laugh and say we need a maintenance bonk to get back on track! It usually works in our relationship."

Most marriages and long-term relationships will have periods when sex is lacking or less frequent. Raising children with all that it requires becomes a distraction and fatigue in the child-bearing years doesn't help. Getting enough sleep is important. If we're tired sex can be the last thing we want. The menopause often affects desire and body confidence and physical changes in the vagina can cause sex to be painful (see below).

Hormone changes at the beginning of the perimenopause phase can result is a real boost to libido for some women. This can be a welcome boost to a marriage where sex may have become less frequent. The best advice is to make the most of it— it may not last but could provide the stimulus for closer relationships and intimacy for the longer term.

What are the obstacles/issues?

There's increasing research into women's sexuality and age. The key findings include the availability of a suitable partner and the quality of the relationship with that person, the woman's previous sexual behaviour, alongside their physical and psychological health as all being important in affecting a woman's sexuality in mid-life. While the physical pain that is often experienced through perimenopause and into menopause affects frequency of sexual activity—especially intercourse—it is how we feel about our partner and our general emotional well-being that have been identified as the strongest predictors of sexual health.

Women told me that everyday distractions and stress will affect sexual frequency. Juliana told me: "It takes time for me to get in the mindset for sex. I cannot just switch it on when there's a space in the day. I have so much stuff in my head about my mum and how she is getting on, my son and his life, the home. To be honest, I want to be wooed gently and make sex an occasion."

If you have been married or in a relationship for a long time, say twenty years or more, and you are conscious that sex is drifting away like a distant sailboat, or a boat that is stuck in the harbour, you need to be honest with yourself about what sort of sexual partner you want to be. It doesn't seem to matter if you and your partner have different sexual drives, what's important is talking about it and maintaining physical intimacy (not necessarily including intercourse) and a mutual appreciation. Sex therapists claim that if you are experiencing problems in your relationship, it's often to do with sex, or lack of it. And that one of the ways that you can help heal a fractured relationship is time spent in bed together just being conscious of each other, building a warm feeling and confidence in one another that builds up to arousal. Some women told me that so-called *Date Nights* work for the benefit of their sexual well-being. By having a time or day in the diary once a month or once a week, it's a signal that both people in the relationship acknowledge the need to be together away from the everyday. This can also be the prelude to sex.

What happens in a sexless marriage/partnership?

The Finnish anthropologist and early sociologist Edvard Westermarck suggested that human beings have an innate tendency to lose desire for people they live with in close quarters over a long period of time if sex is absent. Being very liberal for his time, writing in the 19th century, he was one of the earliest authors to address same-sex relations. The *Westermarck effect* as it became known is the explanation given by some psychologists to explain that a lack of sex in a relationship leads to couples behaving like siblings. Westermarck suggested that this is the natural basis for the incest taboo. Behave like siblings in a relationship and the incest taboo will take effect. You stop having sex over a long period, getting out of the habit and eventually you lose the desire completely. While this is a controversial theory, it makes sense; it's difficult to start to have sex with a partner after a prolonged dry patch, you will need to build up to full intimacy over time.

Problems arise too if one partner wants sex, but the other person actively refuses. Week after week, year after year. Is this fair? What happens instead if you offer your partner the freedom to sleep with someone else "To keep him happy" as one woman told me. "As long as everything stays the same, we preserve the marriage and everything it stands for, I let him have the odd dalliance. He's away a lot so I don't need to know. And what I don't know I don't care about."

This type of collusion in an affair may be the remedy for some but many therapists highlight that having a so-called "free pass" can result in problems. In theory sex with a nameless body, something purely physical is harmless but a sexual liaison with a real human being can lead to intimacy and emotional connection, particularly if the sex with the other person becomes a habit or a regular occurrence. I spoke with a female escort about this and her experiences with clients who are in mid-life. She's a sophisticated, attractive and intelligent woman (let's be clear, this person is a clever businesswoman who has made a definite choice about this career pathway) who explained that the majority of her regular middle-aged male clients are looking for companionship and intimacy. "Mostly they want to talk, to feel that someone is interested in them and while they usually want sex because it's not available in other parts of their lives, it is almost a secondary part of the liaison. Sex is so available to watch online. They want a real woman to talk to as well." She told me.

There is, of course, the issue of boredom in a marriage, and perhaps having an affair can boost a fragile ego in middle age. As we get older, we may want to feel desired and not to feel redundant as a sexual being which may stimulate cheating or infidelity. This applies to men *and* women. Perhaps we want it known that we are desirable. Some people who cheat are not very discreet and I wonder if a wider acknowledgement of desirability is behind this.

One study suggests that men are more likely to cheat with someone they know, which is why affairs at work are common. I have seen all too often men in middle age being tempted by someone at work that responds to him with attention, time, interest, appreciation, and the chance to bare his soul. He or she understands the problems at work when his partner can't. I have seen men who were not particularly physically attractive in their youth but who with time, influence and status become more alluring, especially to younger women or men. Envisage the chap doing well at work, let's call him Joe. He drives a nice car, has the income to buy good clothes and takes care of his appearance. He has grown into his looks. Suddenly Brenda/Tom from Accounts/Sales/IT shows interest. Brenda (or Tom) is gorgeous—the type of girl/boy who would not have given Joe a second glance when he was in his early twenties. He married young, following the trend of his mates from school or university and then out of nowhere, in his forties and fifties he's really desirable. Sex at home has become irregular or infrequent. And before he knows it, he's in a relationship. In many cases once the sexual interest is acted upon, judgement is clouded and there's an illusion that the affair can exist alongside marriage and family life. His happiness seems based on the view that nothing will change at home, but of course it always does.

This scenario can equally apply to a woman being unfaithful with someone at work. Interestingly, couples' counsellors have identified a different behaviour in those women who cheat. Women in long-term relationships often cheat because they want to feel sexually desirable and special, to forget about home, routine and caring responsibilities. They want casual sex to add some spice to life, without complications, and this is something that is not often discussed.

Couples' counsellors tend to recommend avoiding such high-risk strategies for either partner. Instead, they recommend using therapy to improve communication so that the issues behind a need to have affairs or to cheat can be aired and understood. If you can make changes and improvements in the relationship through better communication, very often sex will follow too. Happiness or at least greater contentment all round.

Vaginal dryness and painful sex

The menopause contributes to a lessening of desire in women, often because the natural lubrication in the vagina that helps ensure sex is pleasurable lessens with hormone decline (see chapter on health). The walls and linings of the vagina also get thinner so penetration can be more difficult and painful. Taking time over foreplay can help and lots of lubrication helps too, either through gels or similar, or by taking HRT. HRT treatments typically increase natural lubrication and help most women who have experienced vaginal dryness. Vaginal oestrogen can be used as an alternative which is typically a cream or pessary placed inside the vagina. The advantage of pessaries is the alleviation of vaginal dryness without any of the risks associated with HRT. Note that it will not help with other symptoms of the menopause such as hot flushes. Ask your doctor or go to a menopause clinic for more advice. I cannot emphasise how important this is. You are unlikely to be enthusiastic about sex if it's a painful experience.

Sex and the single woman in mid-life

Much of the research I have included here refers to couples, but as divorce statistics indicate an increase in marriage/relationships breakdown for women in their fifties and older, there are a growing number of singletons who may want to enjoy a fulfilling sex life.

The rules of dating may have changed, as discussed in an earlier chapter, but if you are single and seeking a partner, you need to have a view on sex. If you want a platonic friendship—a companion—it may be a good idea to make this clear to the prospective partner at an appropriate time. If, however, your desires are more at the other end of the scale meaning sex without obligations, this is not surprising. Perhaps you are not ready for a relationship again, possibly you are more experienced, and you want to have fun and enjoy sex for what it is—just sex. Many women report lower inhibitions in mid-life through increased confidence, a greater understanding of themselves, and sex. Years of information about sex in the media and in general conversation has resulted in less stigma about sex than ever before. In a survey about mid-life dating and sex (in both men and women) published by the Sunday Times Style in 2020, only 25% of mid-life singletons revealed that they were now looking to get married and 53% reported that they were open to dating without commitment. 68% of those surveyed revealed that they were more adventurous now than when they were younger.

Sexually transmitted diseases are increasing in the over fifties

A word of caution. A number of reports have shown that sexually transmitted diseases are increasing across the world in people mid-life and over, doubling in the past ten years. In the UK, Canada and the US increasing numbers of fifty- to ninety-year-olds have been diagnosed with syphilis, chlamydia, gonorrhoea and genital herpes.

The number of HIV infections is rising among older people globally because those aged over fifty have not been targeted in messaging and information campaigns about the infection and its consequences. This is also the consequence of people over fifty having more sex, coming out of long-term relationships and literally throwing caution to the wind possibly encouraged by the availability of drugs such as Sildenafil (Viagra).

Women in the post-menopausal years are more vulnerable to STIs because of physical changes to the vagina (see chapter on health). Whatever your age you should seek advice about sexual health, how to practise safe sex. You must use a condom with a new partner. Just because you may be beyond the child-bearing period of your life, you still need to take precautions to stay healthy.

If erectile dysfunction is an issue, there are increasing numbers of pharmaceutical products that can help couples with performance. Men's sexual health can be affected by prostate cancer and diabetes too. The problem is that sexual dysfunction can affect other parts of men's lives, leading to a lack of confidence and even affect decision-making, so keep talking and be open with your partner.

Give me the good news!

We know that mid-life can be very liberating and for some couples the freedom of not having to worry about contraception and unplanned children helps libido. And for some women post-menopause provides clarity of thought and an opportunity to be a little more selfish, using more time and freedom from caring responsibilities to rethink life, and sex can be part of this. Many therapists advocate that a change in thinking may help us to reinvigorate our sex lives. By changing the script, from older women who are not supposed to be sexual beings to a narrative where women can find new levels of pleasure may help us to rediscover and explore our sexual energy as we age.

Research also shows that satisfying sexual behaviour in mid-life, and as women get older, may be more focused on kissing and intimate touching relative to penetrative intercourse for some.

We should also acknowledge that for some women, the biological and psychological changes experienced in mid-life seem to be conducive to alternative sexual experiences. There is much wider understanding that sexual orientation is not fixed and may be flexible. A study of women who identified as heterosexual through early adulthood or later and then experienced "destabilizing" same sex attraction that affected their sense of identity, suggested that societal norms create major obstacles for those wishing to change sexual orientation, especially those in heterosexual marriages with children. Let's hope that this bias can be overcome with better understanding.

The American Psychologist Lisa Diamond was the first to study a large group of women over time and argues that for some, love and desire are not rigidly heterosexual or homosexual but fluid, changing as women move through the stages of life, through social groups and relationships.

Seesaw of allure

Many people see a marked difference between men and women aged fifty and over in terms of perceived allure. Put in a different way, men are deemed to be more attractive than women in mid-life, whereas women are more attractive in their younger years compared with men. Hence the idea of a seesaw. Unfortunately, there is some empirical evidence to back this up; men and women age differently largely due to the marked decline in hormones after menopause (particularly oestrogen, see chapter on health and research on comparative facial ageing after menopause). A study about online dating that reviewed 186,000 messages between straight men and women revealed that men's desirability peaks at age 50, but women's desirability peaks at age 18 and falls throughout their lifespan.

Before you scream at the page that you know lots of women in their fifties, sixties and even seventies who are gorgeous, fit and do not look old, and you know lots of men who have let themselves go with paunches, sagging knees and receding hairlines, let's explore this further. What exactly do we mean by perceived allure or how attractive we are to others? Most of us know that attractiveness is very often determined by more than the physical aspects of a body and face, even though the initial reaction to another person may often by physical. We accept that men, as they age, very often gain experience, influence and status that contribute to an allure that is different from women. Women, like it or not, throughout our lives are more often categorised or assessed by our physical appearance. This difference in perceived attractiveness is demonstrated by older men attracting young women. This is nothing new. We all know or see young women who are attracted to or have been attracted to older men. We are not surprised by this. It may be something you have experienced personally. We may explain it by citing differences in relative income or say that the young woman has what one woman claimed to me was "Daddy issues", the idea that an older man resembles or reminds a young woman of a father figure or older male relative.

Does this seesaw of allure affect our happiness? We may feel that the ageing process makes us vulnerable, feeling less attractive, being invisible. What is commonly thought to be sexy, and desirable is very often linked to youth and youthfulness. Society and the wider media spectrum (and I include online, social media and film in this) commonly celebrates youth and this, women tell me, makes them feel irrelevant in middle age.

Body image and confidence

"Why would anybody find me sexy?" said Martina who is newly divorced and fifty-three. "I look in the mirror and I see saggy boobs and wrinkles." It is true that for many women, once they lose their reproductive ability, their body esteem tends to decline. From an evolutionary perspective being attractive in our younger years signals being available for reproduction— biological fitness is most important when we're young. Some studies have shown a direct relationship between quality of life and body image in mid-age women, and the physical changes that we experience during menopause can contribute towards poor body image. There's some evidence that how satisfied we are with our body may be influenced by personality characteristics such as optimism. If we are already optimistic by nature, we may be less affected by body image and the negative self-perception that others feel more acutely. Research has also found that vulnerability to mental disorders, such as anxiety, may be associated with how positive or negative we feel about the future. If we don't see our future as particularly bright, and we are generally pessimistic then we may feel more anxious about body image. Seeing images of others' perfect lives on social media can only exacerbate feelings of inadequacy in this context so try to avoid if you feel vulnerable.

Building confidence is the answer. Confidence is not something illusive or something you are born with, it's a result. It's a belief that includes skills, self-awareness and behaviours that go beyond the physical aspects of ageing. Sports psychologists say that confidence turns sporting potential into superior performance, and they recommend thinking as a confident person as opposed to feeling confident. Self-confidence can be defined as an assessment of your self-worth and, unsurprisingly, it has a big effect on your happiness. The psychologist Albert Bandura talks about the concept of *Self-efficacy*. He defines this as "The belief in one's capabilities to organize and execute the sources of action required to manage prospective situations." This is closely related to the discrepancy between your self-image (how you see yourself) and your ideal self (how you would ideally like to be). The bigger the gap, the less confident you are. A lack of confidence, or being under-confident, will prevent you from taking risks, from accepting new challenges and from trying new things, like going beyond your comfort zone.

Being confident is sometimes linked to success on the basis that the more successful you are, the more it builds your confidence, sometimes called the circle of success. We need to build in some reality here, high self-confidence is a result of a realistic assessment of your chance of success which is followed by the right outcomes—perhaps your performance or achievement—that matches or exceeds your expectations. There is a limitation, however, as over-confidence can lead to failure. If we overestimate our skills, we may not prepare adequately which may mean we perform poorly. And of course, confidence is not ever increasing, it depends on external factors too, how our health and emotional state are.

Fortunately, discoveries in neuroscience and psychology show that it is possible to amend our thought patterns to build confidence and self-belief: with time and practice we can reduce self-critical and doubting thoughts and reinforce more supportive ones.

Chapter 7
Money, envy, failure and resilience

Does money bring happiness? This is a question pondered by experts over many years. Research suggests that while a lack of money makes you unhappy, having huge wealth does not bring happiness relative to the amount of money you have at your disposal.

When you are struggling to pay everyday bills, the rent or a mortgage, your happiness is usually affected. Not having enough money means we pay attention to these issues. In poorer economies especially, greater income brings increased happiness. We recognise that those people who are well-off financially are, on average, happier than poorer people. Money provides options and a certain amount of freedom.

One of my interviewees summed it up like this: "I have a big issue with people saying, 'Oh, money doesn't make you happy.' Because I think it does. I don't think it answers everybody's problems. It doesn't make everybody healthy. It doesn't buy the perfect relationship. It doesn't buy the perfect children, but it gives you choices."

It seems that having huge amounts of wealth will not make you enormously happy, however. Studies have examined the lives of lottery winners and while there is greater contentment, they do not claim significantly increased and long-term happiness compared with those who haven't won money. One study found that day-to-day happiness levels increase in line with having more money, but only until you hit a certain amount—

about seventy-five thousand dollars a year or fifty-eight thousand pounds. After people earn ninety-five thousand dollars (approx. seventy-four thousand pounds) a year, emotional well-being and life satisfaction start to decline. Studies have found that having a high income brings a greater satisfaction with life but not happiness. It's those things like health, caring for others and loneliness that will predict how happy or contented we are on a day-to-day basis, and not money. Low income particularly affects our life satisfaction, however.

The effect of money on happiness also seems to diminish as we age. In one study based on US based adults, it was shown that money, based on household income, had a significantly smaller effect on happiness for older adults than for young or middle-aged adults.

A study on spending habits revealed that how people spend their money may be at least as important as how much money they earn. Spending your money on other people seems to have more positive impact on happiness than spending money on oneself. There's a lot of interest from researchers in the difference between spending money on material possessions—tangible objects or products that we possess, compared with spending to acquire life experiences. Generally, experiences seem to be more happiness promoting that material possessions. Recent research suggests that it is when experiences are shared with others—think of a holiday with family or friends or a shared day out—that are most likely to support our happiness, and that solitary experiences are less rewarding. It could be that material possessions are more prone to solitary use and this distinction may account for the differential effects on happiness.

Being thrifty, or more careful about how we spend our discretionary income, may also promote life satisfaction. Thrift is less frequently studied in consumer research, but a recent study has shown that spending and consuming less may promote our happiness. It could be that recent consumer trends linked to the negative aspects of over consumption and its effect on climate change may be supporting the satisfaction derived from recycling, upcycling, consumer product exchange programmes and similar.

Rather than how much money we have, it can be the comparison of our wealth against others' that makes us unhappy. I know from interviewing highly successful people about their happiness that the drive to earn more money is often motivated by wanting more than the next person. This is particularly obvious in high performing individuals. It isn't the money itself that is the driver, although obvious manifestations of wealth support feelings of accomplishment, it's that you have more than your rival. And you could demonstrate this by buying a bigger house, a more luxurious car or a boat. Beware, knowing how much your friend or neighbour earns (especially if they earn much more than you) can make you unhappy with your own circumstances.

Caroline, one of the women I interviewed about happiness summed this up very well: "I do think that, quite often, it's not actually about the amount of money. It's the comparison of looking at someone else and their income. And that really is… the death of joy."

Interestingly, happy people earn more money and perform better in the workplace. Numerous studies show that happy people are more content at work than less happy people, and happy people receive more favourable evaluations from managers. So, work on your overall happiness and you may see the results in your job and pay packet. This makes sense. If we are distracted by problems at home or in the wider family, we may not be at our best in the workplace.

Money is clearly not the only goal jobwise. We gain a sense of identity from our jobs and status as well as stimulation and companionship. People who work in the arts or in the charity sector where pay is comparatively low do not report lower levels of happiness than other job sectors. In fact, the reverse is true. Some studies show that non-profit workers both in the UK and the US are generally more satisfied with their jobs than those working for profit-oriented organisations.

This issue is related to purpose and many people say that being part of or contributing to something bigger than themselves as individuals at work contributes to their well-being. Being part of a team that creates something new, solves problems or helps others can bring a sense of meaning. Greater purpose seems to be linked to greater self-esteem, positive perceptions of the world and personal happiness.

Being in control

Being in control of one's life and circumstances seems to matter too. One of my interviewees said this: "I'm in control of what I do... I think that that is extremely important for happiness, it's human nature."

Lack of control, not having enough money or being in a situation where your choices are affected by external factors can make life highly stressful and affect your well-being. Generally, we are happier when we know what to expect from our lives. Having a few surprises can make life interesting but most people like to know that they can pay the rent or the mortgage, that the route to work is predictable or that our families are settled. One woman explained her feelings about times when she was not in control: "One of the key definitions of stress is when things are out of your control, or you don't feel in control. And so, in those times, it's very difficult to feel positive."

Being aware of how much control you prefer may help. Studies show that individuals who report having higher than average daily control also experience greater than average happiness. Equally some people seem to operate in much more relaxed circumstances and periods of loss of control affect their happiness less. Knowing what suits you, in terms of being in control may help you feel happier on a day-to-day basis.

Accept the things you cannot control. Ask yourself if your expectations are sometimes too high. Creating unnecessary stress because things haven't happened in the way you would wish will not contribute to your happiness or those around you. Focus instead on achievements and positive outcomes.

How much self-control one has is often related to positive outcomes in life. Those who have high self-control tend to have better health and do better in an academic sense. New research also relates self-control to life satisfaction. The theory is that we developed self-control to ensure survival. Being able to go without an immediate pleasure for a long-term goal may cause conflict (should I have one more drink now or avoid it to feel better in the morning, for example). Those of us with high self-control may experience greater happiness by fulfilling the more virtuous goal (feeling great in the morning).

Trade-offs

Something that comes up on a regular basis with highly successful individuals is the notion of trade-offs, the sacrifices they make to work a sixty-to-eighty-hour week for example, and how this impacts, on happiness. Many of the senior executives I interviewed in a piece of research about happiness and success revealed that they prioritised the job ahead of family and hobbies. They sacrificed family time, particularly with children. These sacrifices, while expressed in terms of regret and resentment or guilt, are frequently rationalised or justified. As we age many of us will recognise other trade-off behaviour. Many women make trade-offs in terms of their own career progression for the sake of family happiness, for example.

We often face difficult choices in life. Research shows that we trade-off happiness with income, family, career success and education. Our happiness (however it is defined) is more important to most people compared with nearly all other aspects of our lives, except health. The research indicates that we want to feel good rather than have higher life satisfaction or feel more worthwhile in this type of trade-off.

Envy

It seems to me that envy is not a route to happiness. Recent studies into Facebook use have shown that passive following exacerbates feelings of envy which affects how we feel about life—decreasing life satisfaction. Seeing the supposed perfect lives of other people, those we know vaguely, or don't know at all, can make us feel inadequate. It is different when we know the people involved. We may know that a fabulous Instagram photo from an idyllic Mediterranean holiday is the result of hard work and much saving financially to fund the trip, or that underneath there's sadness in the family. We understand the need to show a positive side of life, to cope and carry on. Long before the internet people were putting on their best clothes to go out or go to church. Anyone who has been people-watching in an Italian or Spanish square on a summer evening will see the parade of people dressed up and showing off. It is part of human nature to watch others whether in person or on the internet. We just need to put it all into context and remember that images online are very often enhanced and designed to put a positive spin on situations.

We could all be fitter, thinner, more influential, and wealthier, have more successful children (or husbands/partners) and it's good to aspire to greater things, but constantly measuring ourselves against others is not a route to happiness.

Gratitude and happiness

There is an increasing understanding of the relationship between gratitude and happiness levels. Experiments have shown that grateful thinking or an appreciation of the positive aspects of life improves mood. There's also evidence that gratitude, feeling grateful for things or people and the benefits one has received, can trigger positive emotions, and even build coping abilities. I have mentioned how altruism, helping others, supports well-being. This idea is along the same lines but taking the next step, being thankful for another person's altruism or support. Research seems to suggest that such thinking can support good mental health and even help in the recovery from illness. Gratitude has been shown in medical research to predict lower depression in those with chronic illnesses. Keeping a gratitude diary or journal where you record things you are grateful for on a daily basis has been shown to improve sleep, build resilience, support positive relationships, purpose in life, and self-acceptance. This is not the same as optimism. Gratitude habits orient us towards noticing the positive outcomes in life, whereas optimism is oriented towards the expectation of positive future outcomes.

There are some caveats, however, and while gratitude is at the heart of much of positive psychology literature, the reason that being grateful helps to support feelings of life satisfaction is still not understood. This will not work for everyone all the time and is unlikely to be effective on people who have suffered great poverty or discrimination across their lives. This is what some psychologists call the "dark side of gratitude". Moreover, if you force people to be grateful in the wrong circumstances it can result in feelings of failure and hopelessness. There are situations where it won't work. Think about being in an abusive relationship as an example of this. Trying to cope by being grateful for small things in the relationship will tie you to the abuser when the best outcome would be to seek help and support to leave.

Failure

Your future happiness is better supported if you try to forget failures and past problems. Learning to fail better is a good strategy for life in general and remember that by the time you reach your fifties it is normal to have failed a few times. Focusing on failures can stop us from trying new things, starting new relationships, and making the changes we may need to support a contented later life.

Some people seem to be able to put failures behind them, learning from the experience, rapidly being able to move on. There's no doubt that confronting failures, evaluating what could have been done better so that lessons are learned for the future helps. The good news is that we can learn to fail, to take risks, from the behaviours of others around us. The attitudes of those around you, the values and ethos of your place of work or study or in your friendship groups are, in my opinion, enormously influential.

If you work in a place where failure is unacceptable, not

discussed, or at worst hidden, this will obviously affect your attitude to mistakes. Conversely, if you work in an open environment where failing is a defined part of the learning and development process that everyone shares you will gain courage and take risks for the benefit of the team or group. Scientists and engineers know that significant gains are only made by trying, failing and trying again.

How you manage rejection and failure can determine your future success. This is the reason that job interviews so often include questions about managing difficult situations and failures. It is simply to identify those who are comfortable taking risks but can cope and take appropriate action when things don't go to plan.

There's sound reason why we talk colloquially about the *pain of rejection.* Humans share an innate drive to connect with others. We're evolutionarily wired to crave inclusion. This was originally linked with our survival; in prehistoric times, rejection triggered fear. If someone became isolated or was ousted from the group, his or her life would be at risk.

Because the consequences of being rejected were so extreme, our brains and behaviour adapted to avoid disapproval from others. In fact, research has shown that social rejection activates many of the same brain regions involved in physical pain, which helps explains why disapproval stings. Put a person in an MRI machine and ask them to recall a recent rejection and the same areas of the brain are activated as when we experience physical pain.

While some analysis is necessary and desirable following rejection or failure, it is better to avoid lengthy periods of self-deprecation that may dent self-esteem. An honest appraisal of what went wrong is essential for you to prepare for similar situations or to build a strategy for the future. And a logical examination of the context helps. We all know that the selection process for jobs, for example, often comes with a set of requirements and circumstances over which we have no control.

We can build confidence by focusing on the positives, what we offer as an employee or as a friend for example, reaffirming the qualities we have that are valuable. Knowing how to limit the psychological damage of adversity like rejection will help to build resilience and manage attitude to future risk taking.

Past experience will also affect your attitude to risk and your appetite for failure and this is important. You may be less likely to take risks that affect your income if for instance, the main breadwinner of the family has lost his or her job because of the economic downturn during the pandemic, or perhaps the same situation back in the financial crisis of 2008.

Becoming more resilient for improved life satisfaction

We have all faced challenges and adversity by the time we get to mid-life. The very nature of being a human means we are likely to have experienced family problems—divorce, family breakdown, loss of a loved one, perhaps a miscarriage or major illness in a relative. We may have experienced a family member with mental health issues or loss of income through redundancy or unemployment, and many of us will have experienced loneliness and the lack of someone close to discuss problems with or to celebrate life's joys. Missing out on touch also affects us—more than we realise.

Resilience theories suggest that those individuals who manage to navigate adversity in life and maintain high levels of functioning and well-being demonstrate resilience.

It's important that we learn to manage, or make the best of, the challenges we face in life as we are more likely to encounter different types of adversity as we get older. Many psychologists believe that we can learn to become more resilient through an amalgam of abilities, core beliefs, processes and principles to help us face life difficulties. There's a multitude of research about becoming more resilient and broad agreement on the strategies that work to give hope and help you manage stressful times like a global pandemic. Three strategies worth thinking about are:

- Resilient people accept that things go wrong sometimes and that bad times, the tough times, are part of life. If you remember that terrible things happen to everyone, it makes you realise that it's not just you—you are not singled out for life's difficulties. A perfect life is just not the norm.

- Resilient people focus on the things they *can* change, accepting the things they *can't*. Psychologists show that we are hard-wired to remember the bad times. Think of a situation, perhaps a meeting or a presentation or a social event where something went wrong, even a small thing or incident. You will probably remember this incident more than the rest of the event. We're good at noticing negative emotions. This was good from an evolutionary perspective—in prehistoric time we remembered major threats for our very survival. The problem is that now our threat response is set at maximum all the time—everything is a threat at times. Resilient people have worked out a way to focus on the good emotions. Some psychologists call this finding the benefits in life or highlighting the good in life, being grateful for what is good in life, however small.

- Resilient people ask *Is my behaviour helping me or harming me? Is what I am doing helping me to get over loss, my divorce, my broken heart, or making it worse?* This helps you maintain some kind of control, and as shown in this book, being in control helps with happiness.

Chapter 8
Summary

Most of us are living much longer than previous generations. By mid-life we should be looking forward to several more decades of being active and productive. How women manage the ups and downs of life over fifty while managing health challenges, as well as being income generators through longer employment, became a keen area of interest during my recent studies. It is clear to me that women in mid-life represent a new social group, and we need to be prepared to embrace life and be happy.

Reaching your late forties, early fifties and later can be a watershed. It can be a point in life where we reassess and think about what makes us happy, or what could make us happier and more contented as we get older. The best years may still be ahead, but we need to have the courage, inspiration and determination to make changes for improved well-being.

You may use this time to look for variety, new challenges, and a chance for personal growth. This could involve a new job, new relationships and even a new sense of ourselves through a changed identity from a new purpose.

Perhaps this is the time to find new skills through training or go back to college or university and study something that really interests you. It could be the stimulus to find a job for the first time since having children or to search for a different job or push for promotion. Divorce rates in in the over fifties and over sixties are rising. Many influential divorce lawyers in London have told me that this trend is accelerating. It seems that it is frequently women who want a change. It is the women who are deciding to choose a different path for the final decades of their lives.

We cannot deny that obstacles often increase as we age. We can be affected by our own decline in health and the caring responsibilities of older members of the family. We may lack confidence in our appearance or in our abilities—both physical and intellectual—which may prevent us from trying new things, from exploring and investigating possibilities. We may also have to manage the disappointment of others in our family, their challenges at work and struggles in relationships or through bereavement. We may also have to cope with declining income or loss of jobs.

What can you do? Can you choose to be happy?

You need to put in place strategies and practices to support your happiness in later life, to overcome disappointment, to manage declining health and to focus on the future. Focus on what you can change and be determined about it. Focus on now, on this moment. Learn how to live in the present. I am guilty of always planning and anticipating what comes next, forgetting to enjoy the now—it is not the best strategy for a contented life. Some recommend mindfulness as a way of focusing one's awareness on the present while calmly acknowledging and accepting one's feelings, thoughts, and bodily sensations. Many say it is particularly good for managing anxiety.

Are some people programmed to be happier?

Being optimistic about life affects our longevity, according to Behavioural Science research. Optimism is defined as a psychological attribute characterised by a general expectation that the future will be favourable and that good things will happen because you can control outcomes. Optimism, what some people may call "a glass half full" outlook on life, has been shown to be associated with an eleven to fifteen per cent longer life span compared with the average person, and this exceptional longevity means we are more likely to live to the age of eighty-five or beyond. What is interesting is that the study found that these results were not related to health behaviours (smoking, diet and alcohol consumption), socio-economic status, depression or how integrated we are in society. So being optimistic seems like a good way to be.

Here are my recommendations for being happy in mid-life:
- Change your behaviour rather than trying to change your thinking. Small acts, changing little things will do more to make you happy than over thinking life's challenges.
- Do something for other people. Research shows that altruism is more effective at making you happy than things like shopping, spa treatments and suchlike (although a little bit of self-care can be good for us too).
- Make sure you spend time with others, developing social relationships beyond the family. Even the most introverted people will gain from activities or jobs which involve interaction with others.
- Work at friendships. Mid-life is a stage when changing social, health, and personal factors can influence the relationship between friendship and our happiness. Take steps to make sure you see people you like and enjoy interacting with.
- Cultivate weak ties, those people we see at the supermarket or in a local café who remember you and chat. These small interactions about everyday things can help to improve well-being—we feel like we belong and that's important even for the

busiest of people.

- Try something new that stimulates you to think about new things and involves meeting other people—join a choir or volunteer for a local charity. Do something where your participation matters. Travelling, exploring new places and meeting new people, can increase our life satisfaction too.

- Get your weight under control and be happy about your body. Choose a healthy diet; the Mediterranean diet seems to best suit us as we age with plenty of fish, vegetables, a little lean meat and less sugar. Stick to it for life.

- Research indicates that choosing red wine over white wine and spirits has beneficial effects on the gut (remember, moderation is key).

- Take regular exercise. If you have not exercised very much since school days, it is never too late to see the benefits. Your heart rate will go down, blood pressure too and you will have more energy, and as an added benefit you will look better. Exercise helps to control menopausal symptoms and promotes general feelings of well-being. Start by regular walking—it works.

- Get help if you are experiencing debilitating menopausal symptoms. Don't feel guilty about seeing your doctor or getting advice from a menopause clinic. If you can't manage the symptoms through a natural approach and need HRT to help, you should not feel that you have failed or embarrassed about seeking different options. Remember menopausal symptoms can last for many years—don't hesitate to get help.

- Have a goal and think about purpose. Pursuing a goal, whether it's an exercise goal, taking a course to get a new skill or starting a new business will help you to take charge of your life. Personal goals have important implications for our happiness.

- Learn how to deal with failure and disappointment. How you see adversity will affect the way you react to situations in the future and by not feeling like a victim you are better disposed to manage the normal ups and downs that affect us all.

- Stop being envious. We could all be fitter, thinner, more influential, and wealthier, have more successful children (or husbands/partners) and it's good to aspire to greater things, but constantly measuring ourselves against others is not a route to happiness.

- Get outside more and gain benefit from natural sunlight, no matter what time of year it is—this is important for vitamin D levels that affects bone health and our blood pressure. Access to sunlight affects our sleep patterns, our immune systems and our mental health. We need sunlight in order to live a happy and fulfilling life.

- Have more sex! Understand that relationships with partners or spouses can benefit from sex, making you closer as well as supporting self-esteem. We know that sexual desire diminishes with age and that effort is often required to maintain regular sexual contact, but it is possible to find new energy and liberate forgotten passions in mid-life.

- Appreciate the natural world, even a walk in the park has been shown to improve life satisfaction.

- Spend your money on experiences rather than material goods. We remember experiences—trips with family or friends—more than material goods because they are shared. We are happiest when we share with others. Material possessions are more prone to solitary use and this distinction may account for the differential effects on happiness.

- Experience the arts to support your well-being; music has the power to transform mood, lifting the spirits. Dance allows you to connect with others, to become aware of your body through exercise and develop musicality. The visual arts have been shown to promote well-being, especially in health-care settings. So try to experience the arts of all kinds to support your physical and mental well-being.

• Be the best version of yourself and then forget about it—being interested in others is the key. You are also more likeable if you listen.

• Pay attention to what makes *you* feel good. Remember your happiness, your life satisfaction is the goal. It will not be the same for other women.

• Be grateful for what's good in your life where you can—gratitude has been shown to improve happiness and mental health.

• Be bold. Be determined to do the things or make the changes needed to make you happy. It can take courage to change an established path or pattern of behaviour and accept that change can take time and many small steps.

• Understand that you are not alone. There are literally millions of women reaching mid-life too, in an era when they can expect to live longer, healthier, more fulfilled lives than those who preceded them.

Finally, there is a growing body of evidence that suggests that psychological and sociological factors have a significant influence on how well individual's age. Research into ageing has demonstrated that a person's religious beliefs, social relationships, perceived health, confidence, and coping skills are associated with the ability to age more successfully. So, while happiness can seem elusive at times, we can ensure we choose pathways, relationships and everyday behaviours that support our well-being and improve life satisfaction. And that is the key to being a happy woman in mid-life.

AH 2020

References by Chapter

Foreword
- Measuring wellbeing and progress, OECD (2020, March) https://www.oecd.org/sdd/OECD-Better-Life-Initiative.pdf
- United Nations. (2020). Policy brief: The impact of COVID-19 on older persons. *United Nations report.*
- Biddlestone, M., Green, R., & Douglas, K. M. (2020). Cultural orientation, power, belief in conspiracy theories, and intentions to reduce the spread of COVID-19. *British Journal of Social Psychology*, *59*(3), 663-673.
- Hone, L. (2017). *Resilient grieving: Finding strength and embracing life after a loss that changes everything.* The Experiment.
- Lockdown loneliness & the collapse of social life at work. (2020, August 18). https://www.totaljobs.com/advice/lockdown-loneliness-the-collapse-of-social-life-at-work
- Pearlman, S. F. (2014). Late mid-life astonishment: Disruptions to identity and self-esteem. In *Faces of women and aging* (pp. 11-22). Routledge.
- Simkin-Silverman, L. R., Wing, R. R., Boraz, M. A., & Kuller, L. H. (2003). Lifestyle intervention can prevent weight gain during menopause: results from a 5-year randomized clinical trial. *Annals of Behavioral Medicine*, *26*(3), 212-220.

Chapter 1: What is happiness and why is it important?

- Alesina, A., Di Tella, R., & MacCulloch, R. (2004). Inequality and happiness: are Europeans and Americans different? *Journal of Public Economics, 88*(9-10), 2009-2042.
- Argyle, M. (2013). *The Psychology of Happiness.* Hoboken: Taylor and Francis.
- Clark, A. E., Flèche, S., Layard, R., Powdthavee, N., & Ward, G. (2019). *The origins of happiness: The science of well-being over the life course.* Princeton University Press.
- Cheng, H., & Furnham, A. (2002). Personality, peer relations, and self-confidence as predictors of happiness and loneliness. *Journal of adolescence, 25*(3), 327-339.
- David, S., Boniwell, I., & Ayers, A. C. (2012). *Oxford handbook of happiness.* OUP Oxford.
- Diener, E., Suh, E. M., Lucas, R. E., & Smith, H. L. (1999). Subjective well-being: Three decades of progress. *Psychological Bulletin, 125*(2), 276-302.
- Dolan, P. (2014). *Happiness by design: Finding pleasure and purpose in everyday life.* Penguin UK.
- Dolan, P. (2019). *Happy ever after: Escaping the myth of the perfect life.* Penguin UK.
- Dolan, P., Peasgood, T., & White, M. (2008). Do we really know what makes us happy? A review of the economic literature on the factors associated with subjective well-being. *Journal of Economic Psychology, 29*(1), 94-122.
- Easterlin, R. A. (1995). Will raising the incomes of all increase the happiness of all? *Journal of Economic Behavior & Organization, 27*(1), 35-47.
- Fleurbaey, M., & Schwandt, H. (2015). Do People Seek to Maximize Their Subjective Well-Being? *IZA Discussion Paper No. 9450.*

- Frijters, P., & Beatton, T. (2012). The mystery of the U-shaped relationship between happiness and age. *Journal of Economic Behavior & Organization, 82*(2-3), 525-542.
- In Mulnix, J. W., & In Mulnix, M. J. (2015). *Theories of happiness: An anthology.*
- Lang, F. R., & Heckhausen, J. (2001). Perceived control over development and subjective well-being: Differential benefits across adulthood. *Journal of Personality and Social Psychology, 81*(3), 509-523.
- Layard, R. (2014). *Happiness: Lessons from a new science.* New York: Penguin Books.
- Levinson, D. J. (1977). The mid-life transition: A period in adult psychosocial development. *Psychiatry, 40*(2), 99-112.
- Walker, A. (2005). 25th volume celebration paper towards an international political economy of ageing. *Ageing and Society, 25*(6), 815-839.
- World Happiness Report. (2018, March 14). World Happiness Report 2018. Retrieved from http://worldhappiness.report/ed/2018/

Chapter 2: Relationships, social interaction, and happiness

- Billings, A. G., & Moos, R. H. (1981). The role of coping responses and social resources in attenuating the stress of life events. *Journal of Behavioral Medicine, 4*(2), 139-157.
- Diener, E., Tay, L., & Myers, D. G. (2011). The religion paradox: If religion makes people happy, why are so many dropping out? *Journal of Personality and Social Psychology, 101*(6), 1278-1290.
- Eichhorn, J. (2011). Happiness for Believers? Contextualizing the Effects of Religiosity on Life-Satisfaction. *European Sociological Review, 28*(5), 583-593.

- Feeling lonely. (2020, August 26). https://www.ageuk.org.uk/information-advice/health-wellbeing/loneliness/how-to-overcome-loneliness/
- Grant, A. M. (2013). Rethinking the Extraverted Sales Ideal. *Psychological Science, 24*(6), 1024-1030.
- Moyer, C. A., Rounds, J., & Hannum, J. W. (2004). A meta-analysis of massage therapy research. *Psychological Bulletin, 130*(1), 3-18.
- Myers, D. G. (2000). The funds, friends, and faith of happy people. *American Psychologist, 55*(1), 56-67.
- Sandstrom, G. M., & Dunn, E. W. (2014). Social Interactions and Well-Being. *Personality and Social Psychology Bulletin, 40*(7), 910-922.
- Singh, A., & Misra, N. (2009). Loneliness, depression and sociability in old age. *Industrial Psychiatry Journal, 18*(1), 51.
- UCL. (2019, March 1). Daily TV linked to memory decline in over 50s, https://www.ucl.ac.uk/news/2019/feb/daily-tv-linked-memory-decline-over-50s
- Williams, S. (2015). Singing kick starts social bonding. *Science.* https://psychcentral.com/lib/about-oxytocin/

Chapter 3: Family life, marriage, divorce, and happiness

- Asoodeh, M. H., Khalili, S., Daneshpour, M., & Lavasani, M. G. (2010). Factors of successful marriage: Accounts from self-described happy couples. *Procedia—Social and Behavioral Sciences, 5*, 2042-2046.
- Brown, S. L., & Lin, I. (2012). The Gray Divorce Revolution: Rising Divorce Among Middle-Aged and Older Adults, 1990-2010. *The Journals of Gerontology Series B: Psychological Sciences and Social Sciences, 67*(6), 731-741.

- Diener, E., Gohm, C. L., Suh, E., & Oishi, S. (2000). Similarity of the Relations between Marital Status and Subjective Well-Being Across Cultures. *Journal of Cross-Cultural Psychology*, *31*(4), 419-436.

- Glenn, N. D., & McLanahan, S. (1981). The Effects of Offspring on the Psychological Well-Being of Older Adults. *Journal of Marriage and the Family*, *43*(2), 409.

- Helland, M. S., Von Soest, T., Gustavson, K., Røysamb, E., & Mathiesen, K. S. (2014). Long shadows: a prospective study of predictors of relationship dissolution over 17 child-rearing years. *BMC Psychology*, *2*(1).

- Hewitt, B., Baxter, J., & Western, M. (2005). Marriage breakdown in Australia. *Journal of Sociology*, *41*(2), 163-183.

- Lassale, C., Batty, G. D., Baghdadli, A., Jacka, F., Sánchez-Villegas, A., Kivimäki, M., & Akbaraly, T. (2018). Healthy dietary indices and risk of depressive outcomes: A systematic review and meta-analysis of observational studies. *Molecular Psychiatry*, *24*(7), 965-986.

- Lauer, R. H., Lauer, J. C., & Kerr, S. T. (2019). The long-term marriage: Perceptions of stability and satisfaction. *The Ties of Later Life*, 35-41.

- Lucas, R. E., Clark, A. E., Georgellis, Y., & Diener, E. (2003). Re-examining adaptation and the set point model of happiness: Reactions to changes in marital status. *Journal of Personality & Social Psychology*, *84*(3), 527-539.

- Luhmann, M., Lucas, R. E., Eid, M., & Diener, E. (2012). The Prospective Effect of Life Satisfaction on Life Events. *Social Psychological and Personality Science*, *4*(1), 39-45.

- Twenge, J. M., Campbell, W. K., & Foster, C. A. (2003). Parenthood and Marital Satisfaction: A Meta-Analytic Review.

Journal of Marriage and Family, *65*(3), 574-583.

- Unhappily ever after: Why bad marriages hurt women's health—CNN.com. (n.d.). http://edition.cnn.com/2009/HEALTH/03/06/marriage.women.h eart/index.html

- Wadsworth, T. (2015). Marriage and subjective well-being: How and why context matters. *Social Indicators Research*, *126*(3), 1025-1048.

- Parents who regret having children, YouGov. (2020, May) https://docs.cdn.yougov.com/i64rier7lv/Parents%20who%20reg ret%20having%20children.pdf

Chapter 4: Health, wellbeing, and happiness

- Alexopoulos, G. S., & Morimoto, S. S. (2011). The inflammation hypothesis in geriatric depression. *International Journal of Geriatric Psychiatry*

- Argyle, M. (1997). Is happiness a cause of health? *Psychology & Health*, *12*(6), 769-781.

- Beute, F., & De Kort, Y. A. (2018). The natural context of wellbeing: Ecological momentary assessment of the influence of nature and daylight on affect and stress for individuals with depression levels varying from none to clinical. *Health & Place*, *49*, 7-18.

- BSc, A. A. (n.d.). The fat-soluble vitamins: A, D, E and K. https://www.healthline.com/nutrition/fat-soluble-vitamins

- Di Paola, M., De Filippo, C., Cavalieri, D., Ramazzotti, M., Poullet, J., Massart, S., … Lionetti, P. (2011). undefined. *Digestive and Liver Disease*, *43*, S445-S446.

- Chilling studies show cold weather could increase stroke risk. (2019, January 31).

https://www.heart.org/en/news/2019/01/31/chilling-studies-show-cold-weather-could-increase-stroke-risk

- Diet and the gut microbiota. (2016, July 5). https://foodandmoodcentre.com.au/diet-and-the-gut-microbiota/

- Dubnov, G., Brzezinski, A., & Berry, E. M. (2003). Weight control and the management of obesity after menopause: The role of physical activity. *Maturitas*, *44*(2), 89-101.

- Chilling studies show cold weather could increase stroke risk. (2019, January 31). https://www.heart.org/en/news/2019/01/31/chilling-studies-show-cold-weather-could-increase-stroke-risk

- Geddes, L. (2019). *Chasing the Sun: The New Science of Sunlight and How it Shapes Our Bodies and Minds*. London, England: Profile Books.

- Groves, M. (n.d.). Menopause diet: How what you eat affects your symptoms. Retrieved from https://www.healthline.com/nutrition/menopause-diet#foods-to-avoid

- Hamer, M., Lavoie, K. L., & Bacon, S. L. (2013). Taking up physical activity in later life and healthy ageing: The English Longitudinal Study of Ageing. *British Journal of Sports Medicine*, *48*(3), 239-243.

- Harvard Health Publishing. (2020, June 17). Outrunning the risk of dementia. https://www.health.harvard.edu/aging/outrunning-the-risk-of-dementia?

- Hughes, L. (2020, July 9). Do you know how your vagina is changing as you age? Retrieved from https://www.womanandhome.com/health-and-wellbeing/vagine-ageing-timeline-changes-30s-60s-92297

- Hurd Clarke, L. (2019). Aging, gender, and the body.

The Oxford Handbook of the Sociology of Body and Embodiment.

• Jafary, F., Farahbakhsh, K., Shafiabadi, A., & Delavar, A. (2011). Quality of life and menopause: Developing a theoretical model based on meaning in life, self-efficacy beliefs, and body image. *Aging & Mental Health, 15*(5), 630-637.

• Kyriopoulos, I., Athanasakis, K., & Kyriopoulos, J. (2018). Are happy people healthier? An instrumental variable approach using data from Greece. *Journal of Epidemiology and Community Health, 72*(12), 1153-1161.

• Lachman, M. E., & Weaver, S. L. (1998). The sense of control as a moderator of social class differences in health and well-being. *Journal of Personality and Social Psychology, 74*(3), 763-773.

• Lobos, G., Grunert, K. G., Bustamante, M., & Schnettler, B. (2015). With health and good food, great life! Gender differences and happiness in Chilean rural older adults. *Social Indicators Research, 127*(2), 865-885.

• Medina, J. (2017). *Brain rules for aging well: 10 principles for staying vital, happy, and sharp.* Pear Press.

• Menopause, British Nutrition Foundation. (n.d.). https://www.nutrition.org.uk/healthyliving/lifestages/menopaus e.html

• Nutsford, D., Pearson, A., & Kingham, S. (2013). An ecological study investigating the association between access to urban green space and mental health. *Public Health, 127*(11), 1005-1011.

• Pae, C. U., Mandelli, L., Kim, T. S., Han, C., Masand, P. S., Marks, D. M., … & Serretti, A. (2009). Effectiveness of antidepressant treatments in pre-menopausal versus post-menopausal women: a pilot study on differential effects of sex hormones on antidepressant effects. *Biomedicine &*

pharmacotherapy, *63*(3), 228-235.

- Red wine benefits linked to better gut health study finds. (2019, August 28). https://www.kcl.ac.uk/news/red-wine-benefits-linked-to-better-gut-health-study-finds

- Richards, J., Jiang, X., Kelly, P., Chau, J., Bauman, A., & Ding, D. (2015). Don't worry, be happy: Cross-sectional associations between physical activity and happiness in 15 European countries. *BMC Public Health*, *15*(1).

- Ryff, C. D., Singer, B. H., & Dienberg Love, G. (2004). Positive health: Connecting well—being with biology. *Philosophical Transactions of the Royal Society of London. Series B: Biological Sciences*, *359*(1449), 1383-1394.

- Van der Rhee, H., De Vries, E., & Coebergh, J. (2016). Regular sun exposure benefits health. *Medical Hypotheses*, *97*, 34-37.

- Five things to know about inflammation and depression https://www.psychiatrictimes.com/special-reports/five-things-know-about-inflammation-and-depression

Chapter 5: Purpose

- How to Support Your Older Workers, CIPD (2019, May) https://www.cipd.co.uk/Community/blogs/b/research-blog/posts/how-to-support-your-older-workers#gref

- Benz, M. (2005). Not for the profit, but for the satisfaction?—Evidence on worker well-being in non-profit firms. *Kyklos*, *58*(2), 155-176.

- Borgonovi, F. (2008). Doing well by doing good. The relationship between formal volunteering and self-reported health and happiness. *Social Science & Medicine*, *66*(11), 2321-2334.

- Börsch-Supan, A., & Schuth, M. (n.d.). Early

Retirement, Mental Health, and Social Networks. *Discoveries in the Economics of Aging*, 225-254.

- Calvo, E., Haverstick, K., & Sass, S. A. (2009). Gradual retirement, sense of control, and retirees' happiness. *Research on Aging*, *31*(1), 112-135.
- Emslie, C., & Hunt, K. (2009). 'Live to Work' or 'Work to Live'? A Qualitative Study of Gender and Work-life Balance among Men and Women in Mid-life. *Gender, Work & Organization*, *16*(1), 151-172.
- Erdogan, B., Bauer, T. N., Truxillo, D. M., & Mansfield, L. R. (2012). Whistle While You Work. *Journal of Management*, *38*(4), 1038-1083
- Fisher, C. D. (2010). Happiness at Work. *International Journal of Management Reviews*, *12*(4), 384-412.
- The happiness advantage: the seven principles of positive psychology that fuel success and performance at work. (2011). *Choice Reviews Online*, *48*(07), 48-4166-48-4166.
- Hooper, J. O., & Traupmann, J. A. (1983). Older women, the student role and mental health. *Educational Gerontology*, *9*(2-3), 233-242.
- How Old Are Successful Tech Entrepreneurs? (2018, May 15). https://insight.kellogg.northwestern.edu/article/younger-older-tech-entrepreneurs
- Hochschild, A. R., & Arlie, H. R. (1997). *The time bind: When work becomes home and home becomes work*. Macmillan.
- Lucas, R., & Diener, E. (2003). The happy worker: Hypotheses about the role of positive affect in worker productivity. *Personality and work*, 30-59.
- Lyubomirsky, S., King, L., & Diener, E. (2005). The Benefits of Frequent Positive Affect: Does Happiness Lead to Success? *Psychological Bulletin*, *131*(6), 803-855.

- Martela, F., & Steger, M. F. (2016). The three meanings of meaning in life: Distinguishing coherence, purpose, and significance. *The Journal of Positive Psychology*, *11*(5), 531-545.

- Ng, E. S., & Law, A. (2013). Keeping up! Older workers' adaptation in the workplace after age 55. *Canadian Journal on Aging / La Revue canadienne du vieillissement*, *33*(1), 1-14.

- Ostrander, S. A. (n.d.). "Surely You're Not in This Just to Be Helpful": Access, Rapport, and Interviews in Three Studies of Elites. *Studying Elites Using Qualitative Methods*, 133-150.

- Roberts, J., Hodgson, R., & Dolan, P. (2011). "It's driving her mad": Gender differences in the effects of commuting on psychological health. *Journal of Health Economics*, *30*(5), 1064-1076.

- Scheier, M. F., Wrosch, C., Baum, A., Cohen, S., Martire, L. M., Matthews, K. A., … Zdaniuk, B. (2006). The life engagement test: Assessing purpose in life. *Journal of Behavioral Medicine*, *29*(3), 291-298.

- Tadic, M., Oerlemans, W. G., Bakker, A. B., & Veenhoven, R. (2012). Daily activities and happiness in later life: The role of work status. *Journal of Happiness Studies*, *14*(5), 1507-1527.

- Walker, H., Grant, D., Meadows, M., & Cook, I. (2007). Women's experiences and perceptions of age discrimination in employment: Implications for research and policy. *Social Policy and Society*, *6*(1), 37.

- Adults to gain new skills on 400 free courses, Dept for Education, UK Government (2020, December) https://www.gov.uk/government/news/adults-to-gain-new-skills-on-400-free-courses

Chapter 6: Sex, attraction, and confidence

- Arie, S. (2010). HIV infection is rising among over 50s across the world, figures how. *BMJ*, *341*(jul27 2), c4064-c4064.
- Bancroft, J., Loftus, J., & Long, J. S. (2003). Distress about sex: A national survey of women in heterosexual relationships. *Archives of sexual behavior*, *32*(3), 193-208.
- Bandura, A. (1982). Self-efficacy mechanism in human agency. *American Psychologist*, *37*(2), 122-147.
- Bandura, A. (1995). Self-efficacy in Changing Societies.
- Bruch, E. E., & Newman, M. E. J. (2018). Aspirational pursuit of mates in online dating markets. *Science Advances*, *4*(8), eaap9815.
- Diamond, L. M. (2015). Sexual fluidity. *The international encyclopedia of human sexuality*, 1115-1354.
- Dennerstein, L., Lehert, P., Burger, H., & Dudley, E. (1999). Factors affecting sexual functioning of women in the mid-life years. *Climacteric*, *2*(4), 254-262.
- Fleishman, M. R. (1992). *Sexuality is not fixed: A study of thirty heterosexual women whose sexual orientation changed at mid-life* (Doctoral dissertation, Saybrook University).
- Francis, D. (2008). *Partners in passion*. D & J Holdings LLC.
- Godson, S. (2013). *The sex book*. Hachette UK.
- Hanton, S., & Connaughton, D. (2002). Perceived control of anxiety and its relationship to self-confidence and performance. *Research quarterly for exercise and sport*, *73*(1), 87-97.
- Jackson, S. E., Yang, L., Koyanagi, A., Stubbs, B., Veronese, N., & Smith, L. (2019). Declines in sexual activity and function predict incident health problems in older adults:

Prospective findings from the English Longitudinal Study of Ageing. *Archives of Sexual Behavior*, *49*(3), 929-940.

- Heiman, J. R., Long, J. S., Smith, S. N., Fisher, W. A., Sand, M. S., & Rosen, R. C. (2011). Sexual satisfaction and relationship happiness in midlife and older couples in five countries. *Archives of Sexual Behavior*, *40*(4), 741-753.

- Magon, N., Chauhan, M., Malik, S., & Shah, D. (2012). Sexuality in midlife: Where the passion goes? *Journal of mid-life health*, *3*(2), 61.

- Moran, C. S. (2008). *Mid-life sexuality transitions in women: A queer qualitative study*. Southern Connecticut State University.

- Nappi, R. E., & Lachowsky, M. (2009). Menopause and sexuality: Prevalence of symptoms and impact on quality of life. *Maturitas*, *63*(2), 138-141.

- Nelson, T. (2012). *Getting the sex you want: Shed your inhibitions and reach new heights of passion together*. Quiver.

- Prairie, B. A., Scheier, M. F., Matthews, K. A., Chang, C. H., & Hess, R. (2011). A higher sense of purpose in life is associated with sexual enjoyment in midlife women. *Menopause*, *18*(8), 839-844.

- Rosen, R. C., & Bachmann, G. A. (2008). Sexual well-being, happiness, and satisfaction, in women: The case for a new conceptual paradigm. *Journal of Sex & Marital Therapy*, *34*(4), 291-297.

- Simson, R. V., & Kulasegaram, R. (2012). Sexual health and the older adult. *BMJ*, e688.

- Slater, A., Cole, N., & Fardouly, J. (2019). The effect of exposure to parodies of thin-ideal images on young women's body image and mood. *Body Image*, *29*, 82-89.

- Snyder, S. (2019). *Love worth making: How to have*

ridiculously great sex in a long-lasting relationship. St. Martin's Griffin.

- Stokes, R., & Frederick-Recascino, C. (2003). Women's perceived body image: Relations with personal happiness. *Journal of Women & Aging, 15*(1), 17-29.
- Strobel, M., Tumasjan, A., & Spörrle, M. (2011). Be yourself, believe in yourself, and be happy: Self-efficacy as a mediator between personality factors and subjective well-being. *Scandinavian Journal of psychology, 52*(1), 43-48.
- Thomas, H. N., Chang, C. C. H., Dillon, S., & Hess, R. (2014). Sexual activity in midlife women: importance of sex matters. *JAMA internal medicine, 174*(4), 631-633.
- Wadsworth, T. (2013). Sex and the Pursuit of Happiness: How Other People's Sex Lives are Related to our Sense of Well-Being. *Social Indicators Research, 116*(1), 115-135.
- America's generation gap in extramarital sex. (2017, July) https://ifstudies.org/blog/americas-generation-gap-in-extramarital-sex
- An unrecognized reason that married men have affairs. PsychCentral. (2013, September). https://blogs.psychcentral.com/healing-together/2013/09/an-unrecognized-reason-that-married-men-have-affairs/
- The Mid-life Guide to Dating and Sex. Sunday Times. (2020, February) https://www.thetimes.co.uk/article/the-midlife-guide-to-dating-and-sex-rlf00tp50

Chapter 7: Money, envy, and failure
- Adler, M. D., Dolan, P., & Kavetsos, G. (2017). Would you choose to be happy? Trade-offs between happiness and the

other dimensions of life in a large population survey. *Journal of Economic Behavior & Organization, 139*, 60-73.

- Baumeister, R. F., Campbell, J. D., Krueger, J. I., & Vohs, K. D. (2003). Does High Self-Esteem Cause Better Performance, Interpersonal Success, Happiness, or Healthier Lifestyles? *Psychological Science in the Public Interest, 4*(1), 1-44

- Bhattacharjee, A., & Mogilner, C. (2014). Happiness from ordinary and extraordinary experiences. *Journal of consumer research, 41*(1), 1-17.

- Boyce, C. J., Brown, G. D., & Moore, S. C. (2010). Money and happiness: Rank of income, not income, affects life satisfaction. *Psychological science, 21*(4), 471-475.

- Brickman, P., Coates, D., & Janoff-Bulman, R. (1978). Lottery winners and accident victims: Is happiness relative? *Journal of Personality and Social Psychology, 36*(8), 917-927.

- Caprariello, P. A., & Reis, H. T. (2013). To do, to have, or to share? Valuing experiences over material possessions depends on the involvement of others. *Journal of personality and social psychology, 104*(2), 199.

- Chancellor, J., & Lyubomirsky, S. (2014). Money for happiness: The hedonic benefits of thrift. In *Consumption and well-being in the material world* (pp. 13-47). Springer, Dordrecht.

- Cheung, T. T., Gillebaart, M., Kroese, F., & De Ridder, D. (2014). Why are people with high self-control happier? The effect of trait self-control on happiness as mediated by regulatory focus. *Frontiers in Psychology, 5.*

- Dunn, E. W., Gilbert, D. T., & Wilson, T. D. (2011). If money doesn't make you happy, then you probably aren't spending it right. *Journal of Consumer Psychology, 21*(2), 115-

125.

- Dunn, E. W., Aknin, L. B., & Norton, M. I. (2008). Spending money on others promotes happiness. *Science*, *319*(5870), 1687-1688.

- Emmons, R. A. (2007). *Thanks!: How the new science of gratitude can make you happier*. Houghton Mifflin Harcourt.

- Emmons, R. A., Froh, J., & Rose, R. (2019). Gratitude. *Positive psychological assessment: A handbook of models and measures (2nd ed.)*, 317-332

- Hsieh, C. M. (2011). Money and happiness: does age make a difference? *Ageing and Society*, *31*(8), 1289.

- Kahneman, D., & Deaton, A. (2010). High income improves evaluation of life but not emotional well-being. *Proceedings of the National Academy of Sciences*, *107*(38), 16489-16493.

- Kahneman, D. (2006). Would You Be Happier If You Were Richer? A Focusing Illusion. *Science*, *312*(5782), 1908-1910.

- Kahneman, D., & Deaton, A. (2010). High income improves evaluation of life but not emotional well-being. *Proceedings of the National Academy of Sciences*, *107*(38), 16489-16493.

- Larson, R. (1989). Is feeling "in control" related to happiness in daily life? *Psychological Reports*, *64*(3), 775-784.

- Lefcourt, H. M. (1984). Introduction. *Research with the Locus of Control Construct*, 1-4.

- Lee, L. O., James, P., Zevon, E. S., Kim, E. S., Trudel-Fitzgerald, C., Spiro, A., … Kubzansky, L. D. (2019). Optimism is associated with exceptional longevity in 2 epidemiologic cohorts of men and women. *Proceedings of the National Academy of Sciences*, *116*(37), 18357-18362.

- Lyubomirsky, S., Tkach, C., & DiMatteo, M. R. (2005). What are the Differences between Happiness and Self-Esteem. *Social Indicators Research, 78*(3), 363-404.

- Norton, M., Aknin, L., & Dunn, E. (2009). From wealth to well-being: Spending money on others promotes happiness. *PsycEXTRA Dataset.*

- Paradise, A. W., & Kernis, M. H. (2002). Self-esteem and psychological well-being: Implications of fragile self-esteem. *Journal of Social and Clinical Psychology, 21*(4), 345-361.

- Rutledge, R. B., De Berker, A. O., Espenhahn, S., Dayan, P., & Dolan, R. J. (2016). The social contingency of momentary subjective well-being. *Nature communications, 7*(1), 1-8.

- Sirois, F. M., & Wood, A. M. (2017). Gratitude uniquely predicts lower depression in chronic illness populations: A longitudinal study of inflammatory bowel disease and arthritis. *Health Psychology, 36*(2), 122-132.

- Watkins, P. C., Woodward, K., Stone, T., & Kolts, R. L. (2003). Gratitude and happiness: Development of a measure of gratitude, and relationships with subjective well-being. *Social Behavior and Personality: an international journal, 31*(5), 431-451.

- When it comes to happiness, money matters. Pew Research. (2014, October). http://www.pewresearch.org/fact-tank/2014/10/30/when-it-comes-to-happiness-money-matters/

- Wood, A. M., Froh, J. J., & Geraghty, A. W. (2010). Gratitude and well-being: A review and theoretical integration. *Clinical Psychology Review, 30*(7), 890-905.

- Wood, A. M., Maltby, J., Stewart, N., Linley, P. A., & Joseph, S. (2008). A social-cognitive model of trait and state levels of gratitude. *Emotion, 8*(2), 281-290.

Chapter 8 Summary

- Bollen, J., Gonçalves, B., van de Leemput, I., & Ruan, G. (2017). The happiness paradox: your friends are happier than you. *EPJ Data Science*, 6(1), 4.
- Fancourt, D., & Steptoe, A. (2019). The art of life and death: 14 year follow-up analyses of associations between arts engagement and mortality in the English Longitudinal Study of Ageing. *bmj*, 367.
- Layous, K., & Lyubomirsky, S. (2014). The How, Why, What, When, and Who of Happiness. *Positive Emotion*, 472-495.
- Sheldon, K. M., Boehm, J., & Lyubomirsky, S. (2013). Variety is the spice of happiness: The hedonic adaptation prevention model. *Oxford Handbooks Online*.
- The State of Ageing in 2020, Centre for Ageing Better. https://www.ageing-better.org.uk/publications